IBC対訳ライブラリー

# 英語で読む
# グレート・ギャツビー

*The Great Gatsby*

著=F・スコット・フィッツジェラルド
英語解説=出水田隆文

イラスト=Tomoko Taguchi
日本語訳=澤田組

# まえがき

## 『グレート・ギャツビー』が書かれた時代とは

　『グレート・ギャツビー（The Great Gatsby）』は、1920年代のアメリカ、とくにニューヨークで華麗な日々をおくる裕福な若者たちの物語です。

　1918年、ヨーロッパで第一次世界大戦が終結します。

　それは、毒ガスや飛行機、そして機関銃などの残酷な近代兵器が、はじめて本格的に使用された大動乱でした。同時に、大戦中やその直後にドイツやロシア、そしてオーストリアやトルコなど、多くの国で19世紀以前の旧体制が崩壊しました。その大動乱を通して一時代の清算が行われたのです。

　第一次世界大戦中、そして戦後を通し、世界ではふたつの顕著な現象がおきています。

　ひとつは、社会主義革命によって帝政ロシアが崩壊し、世界ではじめて共産主義国が誕生したことです。1922年のソビエト社会主義共和国連邦（ソ連）の成立は、古い時代が終焉したことの象徴として若者に捉えられ、アメリカでも社会主義の影響を受けて人種差別や労働者の権利などの問題に人々の関心が集まりました。

　そして、もうひとつがアメリカの繁栄です。

　今まで世界を牽引していたヨーロッパは、この大戦で壊滅状態となり、アメリカが世界で最も裕福な国にのし上がったのです。

　そんなアメリカでは、旧来の制度に縛られた道徳とは無縁の、かつ血筋や身分ではなく資金のある者が時代を謳歌しました。彼らは自分

の趣味のために大金をつかい、芸術などへの投資も惜しみません。才能ある者は、サロンや街のカフェに集い、芸術論議、社会論議に没頭します。その舞台となったのは、世界最大の債権国となったアメリカの経済の中心地、ニューヨークに他なりませんでした。

　こうしたアメリカの繁栄によって、現代に直接つながる多彩な芸術活動が一世を風靡します。しかし同時に、時代は揺れていました。旧来のキリスト教を基軸とした実直なアメリカ人社会は、禁酒法を生み出しました。1919年から1933年まで、消費のためのアルコール製造、販売などが全面的に禁止されたのです。
　そしてその対極ともいえる自由闊達な都市生活に若者が憧れたのもこの時代でした。彼らは、スピークイージー（Speakeasy）と呼ばれるもぐり酒場に集まり、朝まで酒を飲み、当時脚光を浴び始めたジャズに耳を傾けます。このスピークイージーを運営していたのが大都市に暗躍するマフィアでした。
　ソ連の誕生とアメリカの都市部での若者の活動とはお互い無縁ではありません。社会主義活動に触発され社会運動に興味を持つ者と芸術活動は共に旧体制への訣別という点で共通項があったのです。

　このように、第一次世界大戦の前後で、人々の価値観も大きく変わりました。
　そんな過渡期にあったアメリカ社会、それを象徴したのが地方都市とニューヨークとの対比です。禁酒法をつくり出した昔ながらの価値観に育まれた地方都市出身の若者がニューヨークに集まり、そうした殻に反旗を翻す構造が「グレート・ギャツビー」の物語の中にも見え隠れします。作者のフィッツジェラルド自身が、アメリカ中西部にあるミ

ネソタ州の州都セントポールの出身で、その後ニューヨークで活動しました。

ロストジェネレーション（失われた世代）といわれたフィッツジェラルドの世代。ロストジェネレーションとは、第一次世界大戦を経験した若者のことで、彼らこそ戦後のニューヨークの都市文化を謳歌した人々だったのです。戦争の悲惨さとその後のアメリカの経済的な繁栄が、過去の価値観を否定しながらも、次のものを掴めないまま裕福さの中に漂う、こうした世代を生み出します。

「グレート・ギャツビー」と双璧ともいわれる、アーネスト・ヘミングウエイの「日はまた昇る」には、そうした人々の心理が巧みに描かれています。

それはある意味では、80年代後半のバブルに浮かれていた日本にも似通っています。華麗な都市生活は反面空虚なもので、1929年のウォール街の株の大暴落で、バブルは脆くもはじけてしまいます。

「グレート・ギャツビー」に描かれた人々の生活の中に滲む「無意味で殺伐とした繁栄」の空気は、そんな世界の変化を予感したものだったのかもしれません。

F・スコット・フィッツジェラルド F. Scott Fitzgerald は、1920年代のジャズエイジとよばれる第一次世界大戦後のアメリカでもっとも輝いた作家の一人です。フィッツジェラルドの私生活をのぞけば、彼の妻であり作家でもあるゼルダとの愛憎の日々は有名で、ジャズエイジから大恐慌を経て第二次世界大戦へと世界が揺れ動く中、その恋愛と破綻は時代を象徴したエピソードとして書籍や雑誌に取り上げられました。「グレート・ギャツビー（1925年刊）」は、そんなゼルダと結婚して５年目、彼の絶頂期に発表された作品だったのです。

### ニューヨークとロングアイランド

　作品の舞台となるウエストエッグとイーストエッグと呼ばれる地域は、ロングアイランド（ニューヨーク市の東に向けて大西洋岸に長く延びる島）にあるグレート・ネックという場所をモデルにしています。作者自身、妻のゼルダと共に、ここで暮らしたことがあり、ここに描かれている風景は、多分に自らの経験に基づいたものと言えるかもしれません。

　グレート・ネックのあるロングアイランド中部の北海岸は、静かな入り江が多く、そんな風光明媚な自然に魅せられて、富豪の別荘などが多く建っていた地域です。また、島の東の突端に近いハンプトンズと呼ばれる地域も、成功した芸術家や資産家の多く住む地域として知られており、アメリカでも最も高価な住宅地であるとされています。

　物語に登場するジェイ・ギャツビーや、トムとデイジーのブキャナン夫妻のライフスタイルも、まさにそうした地域で育まれたものに他なりません。

　ニューヨーク市は1898年にマンハッタン島とイーストリバーを挟んだ向かいにあるブルックリン地区とが合併し、現在のニューヨーク市の原型ができました。ロングアイランドの西の端に位置するブルックリン地区の北側は、その後、工場や労働者の住宅地として発展しました。「グレート・ギャツビー」の中で、「悲しげな灰色の一帯」と描写されている地域が出てきますが、これは、労働者の集まる現在のニューヨークの５つの区のひとつクイーンズの当時の様子ではないでしょうか。

　物語に登場する自動車修理工場を経営するジョージ・ウイルソンが

活動していたのは、このクイーンズがモデルの街というわけです。

クイーンズ地区に代表されるロングアイランドの西側は、マンハッタンとハンプトンズなどに代表されるロングアイランド東部に挟まれた地域で、新参者の移民が逞しく生きる産業街です。今でもインドやバングラデシュなどからの移民が集まる地域、アイルランド系の人々やユダヤ系の移民の香りが残る地域、さらには中国や韓国から20世紀後半に渡ってきた人々の生活の場などが複雑に交錯しています。

現在のクイーンズもその人口の半分近くが移民一世とその家族というほどですから、その多様性はアメリカの中でも際立っています。

アメリカは一部の人たちを除いて、ほとんどが貧しい移民です。移民たちが入植し、移住して造られた国なのです。富裕層とはいえ、何世代も特権を享受してきた貴族や王族ではなく、名もない移民が才能とチャンスで富を成した、いわばアメリカンドリームの成功者です。

「グレート・ギャツビー」に描かれる人々は、まさにそんなアメリカ人を代表するキャラクターといえましょう。そして、そんな成功者たちのステータスシンボルとなる地域、それが小説のモデルともなった、ロングアイランドの北海岸一帯だったのです。

## F・スコット・フィッツジェラルド略歴

1896年9月24日に、ミネソタ州の州都であるセントポールに生まれます。母親は厳格なカトリックの家の出身で、アイルランド系移民だった祖父は手広く雑貨店を営み、商業的に成功を収めていました。父は、セントポールで始めた商売がうまくいかず、ニューヨーク北部にあるプロクター&ギャンブルのサラリーマンとしての職を得ます。そのため、家族はニューヨーク州バッファローやシラキュースを行き来する

ことになりますが、1908年には、P&Gでの仕事も失ったため、当時12歳だったフィッツジェラルドと家族はセントポールに戻り、母の相続した家で暮らすことになります。そんなどちらかというとうだつの上がらない父でしたが、詩作に耽るなど、文学的な才があったため、フィッツジェラルドは敬愛していたと言われています。

　フィッツジェラルドは、頭がよく、ハンサムで、野心的な子どもでした。とくに母親は彼に期待をかけ、溺愛しますが、フィッツジェラルド自身はそんな母を嫌っていたようです。フィッツジェラルドの初めての創作は、13歳のときで、作品は学校の新聞に掲載されました。1911年、15歳になると、ニュージャージー州の有名なカトリック校、ニューマン・スクールに入学。そこで手がけた脚本が有名になり、17才（1913年）でニューマン・スクールを卒業すると、特別選抜でプリンストン大学への入学が許されます。有名な演劇クラブであるトライアングルクラブに入ったのもこの頃のことです。この時期に、良家の娘と恋に落ちますが、失恋しています。その後もフィッツジェラルドは、金持ちで美しい、もっぱら社交界の花形のような女性とばかり付きあうようになります。

　1917年にアメリカが第一次世界大戦に参戦するのと同時に大学を中退し、陸軍に入隊します。戦場に行けば、命を落とすかもしれないという不安から、急ぎ「ロマンティク・エゴイスト（The Romantic Egotist）」を書き、出版社スクリブナーズCharles Scribner's Sonsに持ち込みますが、ボツとなり出版には至りませんでした。

　フィッツジェラルドは少尉として、アラバマ州モンゴメリー郊外の

キャンプ・シェリダンの歩兵に配属されます。そこで18歳のゼルダ・セイヤー Zelda Sayreと運命の出会いをします。ゼルダはアラバマ最高裁判所の判事である父のもと、良家の子女として何不自由なく暮らしていました。フィッツジェラルドをして、「アラバマ、ジョージアの2州でゼルダほどの美女はいない」と言わしめた美貌の持ち主でした。1919年に戦争が終わると、フィッツジェラルドはニューヨークの広告代理店に勤めますが、ゼルダはフィッツジェラルドの稼ぐ金だけでは暮らせない、という理由で婚約を解消してしまいます。そのこともあって、数ヵ月で広告の仕事をやめ、セントポールに戻り、彼は再び小説を書きはじめます。

失意のフィッツジェラルドでしたが、実家の屋根裏部屋に引きこもって書いた『楽園のこちら側（This Side of Paradise）』が大ベストセラーとなり、24才のフィッツジェラルドは、若手有望作家として注目を浴びることとなります。小説が発表された1週間後にフィッツジェラルドは、ゼルダとニューヨークで結婚。1921年には、娘のフランシス・スコット・フィッツジェラルドが生まれます。

フィッツジェラルドは、ゼルダの浪費やニューヨークの社交界での奔放で華やかな生活を享受するため、収入のいい短編をたくさん書いて、金を稼ごうとします。乱れた生活で才能を浪費しながら、ゼルダとのばか騒ぎを続けたのです。

1924年、2人は娘を連れ、フランスに移り住みます。そこで20世紀のアメリカ文学を代表する作家の1人として認められるフィッツジェラルドの代表作である、「グレート・ギャツビー」を書くことになります。1925年に出版された「グレート・ギャツビー」の当時の評価は、芳しくなく、売り上げにも結びつきませんでした。この作品が正しく評価されるのは、フィッツジェラルドの死以降でした。

　その後もふたりの荒れた生活は続き、フィッツジェラルドの生活は崩壊していきます。フィッツジェラルドは、アルコール依存症となり、妻のゼルダも統合失調症で30年にはスイスの病院に入院を余儀なくされます。1931年にフィッツジェラルドが先にアメリカに戻りますが、翌年、ゼルダもアメリカに戻りバルティモアのジョンズ・ホプキンス病院に転院します。1934年、苦労の末、4作目となる『夜はやさし(Tender is the Night)』を発表しますが、出版当初から作品に対する評価は芳しくなく、フィッツジェラルドはますます酒に溺れるようになります。

　その後、1937年になると、借金返済のため、フィッツジェラルドはハリウッドに移り住み、シナリオライターとなります。結局、アルコールから抜け出せなかったフィッツジェラルドは、何度か心臓発作に襲われ、1939年から「ラスト・タイクーン(The Love of the Last Tycoon)」の執筆に着手しますが、未完のまま心臓発作で亡くなります。1940年、12月21日、44歳でした。

*参考資料
『グレート・ギャツビー』(新潮文庫)
biography.com
wikipedia.com

# もくじ

**まえがき** ............................................................ 3
**本書の構成** ....................................................... 12

## Part 1  Chapter 1 – Chapter 3 ............................ 13
覚えておきたい英語表現 ................................ 50

## Part 2  Chapter 4 – Chapter 6 ............................ 53
覚えておきたい英語表現 ................................ 82

## Part 3  Chapter 7 – Chapter 9 ............................ 85
覚えておきたい英語表現 .............................. 126

## Part 4  Chapter 10 – Chapter 13 ...................... 129
覚えておきたい英語表現 .............................. 180

## Part 5  Chapter 14 – Chapter 17 ...................... 183
覚えておきたい英語表現 .............................. 220

## 本書の構成

本書は、

- □ 英日対訳による本文
- □ 覚えておきたい英語表現
- □ 欄外の語注
- □ MP3形式の英文音声

で構成されています。本書は、アメリカ文学を代表する小説のひとつである『グレート・ギャツビー』をやさしい英語で書きあらためた本文に、日本語訳をつけました。

各ページの下部には、英語を読み進める上で助けとなるよう単語・熟語の意味が掲載されています。また左右ページは、段落のはじまりが対応していますので、日本語を読んで英語を確認するという読み方もスムーズにできるようになっています。またパートごとに英語解説がありますので、本文を楽しんだ後に、英語の使い方などをチェックしていただくのに最適です。

## 付属のCD-ROMについて

本書に付属のCD-ROMに収録されている音声は、パソコンや携帯音楽プレーヤーなどで再生することができるMP3ファイル形式です。一般的な音楽CDプレーヤーでは再生できませんので、ご注意ください。

### ■音声ファイルについて

付属のCD-ROMには、本書の英語パートの朗読音声が収録されています。本文左ページに出てくるヘッドホンマーク内の数字とファイル名の数字がそれぞれ対応しています。

パソコンや携帯プレーヤーで、お好きな箇所を繰り返し聴いていただくことで、発音のチェックだけでなく、英語で物語を理解する力が自然に身に付きます。

### ■音声ファイルの利用方法について

CD-ROMをパソコンのCD/DVDドライブに入れて、iTunesなどの音楽再生(管理)ソフトにCD-ROM上の音声ファイルを取り込んでご利用ください。

### ■パソコンの音楽再生ソフトへの取り込みについて

パソコンにMP3形式の音声ファイルを再生できるアプリケーションがインストールされていることをご確認ください。

CD-ROMをパソコンのCD/DVDドライブに入れても、多くの場合音楽再生ソフトは自動的に起動しません。ご自分でアプリケーションを直接起動して、「ファイル」メニューから「ライブラリに追加」したり、再生ソフトのウインドウ上にファイルをマウスでドラッグ&ドロップするなどして取り込んでください。

音楽再生ソフトの詳しい操作方法や、携帯音楽プレーヤーへのファイルの転送方法については、ソフトやプレーヤーに付属のマニュアルで確認するか、アプリケーションの開発元にお問い合わせください。

# Part 1

# I

When I was younger, my father gave me some advice that I never forgot. He said to me, "If you ever feel like criticizing anyone, just remember that not everybody has had the advantages you have had." That was all he said, but it was enough for me to understand. I took that advice seriously. So, all my life I have listened to people without judging them. Many people realized I was a good listener and told me all about their problems — even things I didn't want to hear about. Finally, after hearing so many people's deepest, darkest secrets, there came a point when I didn't want to listen to other people anymore. I wanted to be left alone.

Gatsby, who I named this book after, was the only exception. Gatsby was one of the most interesting people I ever met. He was full of hopes and dreams. I respected that, even though I didn't agree with most of the things he did.

■if someone ever もし〜なら ■feel like 〜したいと思う ■have an advantage 優位である ■take that advice その忠告に従う ■there comes a point 〜ということがある ■leave alone 独りにしておく ■even though 〜にも関わらず

# I

　僕がまだ若かった頃、父からある忠告をもらった。その忠告を僕は決して忘れたことがない。「人を批判したくなったら、誰もがお前みたいに恵まれているわけではないことを思い出しなさい」 父はそれしか言わなかったが、僕にはじゅうぶん理解できた。僕はその忠告をしっかりと受け止め、以来ずっと、予断を持たずに相手の話を聞くようにしてきた。おかげで少なからぬ人たちから聞き上手だと思われ、あらゆる悩みを打ち明けられた。なかには聞きたくないような話もあった。そうして人のいちばん深く暗い秘密をさんざん聞きつづけてきたあげく、もうこれ以上、他人の話は聞きたくないというところまで来てしまった。1人きりでいたいと思った。

　この本の題名にした人物、ギャツビーだけは例外だ。ギャツビーは、僕が出会ったなかでもとりわけ興味深い人間の1人だ。彼には夢と希望がいっぱいあり、僕はその点を尊敬していた。彼のやることのほとんどには賛同できなかったけれど。

I come from a family of successful businessmen. They all live in the Midwest. I went to college in New Haven, then I joined the army to fight in WWI. When I returned to America, I felt bored and useless, so I decided to become a New York stockbroker. Everyone was becoming a stockbroker in those days, so I thought I would do it too. I moved out to the East Coast in 1922.

I decided to live in a little house on Long Island, in the countryside just outside of New York City. I took the train to the office everyday. My house was located where two hills that look like huge eggs stuck out into the bay. They were called West Egg and East Egg. The two pieces of land were shaped exactly alike, but the lives led on each egg were very different.

I lived at West Egg, which was the less fashionable of the two. My little house was built in between two huge mansions. The one on my right was the bigger mansion, with a swimming pool and a lawn that seemed to go on forever. That was Gatsby's house. I didn't know Gatsby at the time, but I knew a man named Gatsby lived there. Across the bay at East Egg lived my cousin Daisy and her husband Tom. Tom was known as one of the best football players of his time when he was in college at New Haven. He came from a very rich family. He often spent money in a way that shocked people.

■Midwest 名アメリカ中西部　■in those days その当時は　■move out 引っ越す　■stick out 突き出る　■mansion 名豪邸　■seem to 〜のように見える　■go on 続く

僕の家系には財をなした実業家がたくさんいて、みんな中西部に住んでいる。僕は（東部の）ニューヘイブンにある大学に行き、それから軍隊に入って第一次世界大戦で戦った。アメリカに帰還すると、退屈なうえに自分が役立たずのような気がして、ニューヨークで株式ブローカーをやることにした。あの頃はみんなが株のブローカーになっていたから、それなら僕も、と思ったのだ。東海岸へ移住したのは1922年のことだった。

　僕はロングアイランド（ニューヨーク市のすぐ隣にあるのんびりした場所だ）の小さな家に住むことに決めた。職場へは毎日、電車で通った。家は入り江に突き出た巨大な2つの卵のような形の高台に建っていた。2つの高台は、それぞれウェスト・エッグ、イースト・エッグと呼ばれている。地形は瓜二つだが、卵の上の暮らしぶりはまるで違っていた。

　僕が住んでいたのはウェスト・エッグ、イーストほどお洒落ではない。僕の小さな家は2軒の大邸宅に挟まれていた。右側の邸宅はひときわ大きく、プールと果てしなく続く芝生の庭がある。これがギャツビーの家だった。当時は面識がなかったが、ギャツビーという人が住んでいることは知っていた。入り江の向こう側のイースト・エッグには、いとこのデイジーと夫のトムが住んでいた。トムは、ニューヘイブンでの大学時代、その名を轟かせたフットボールの名選手だった。ものすごく裕福な家の出身で、金遣いの荒さは周りをしばしば驚かせたものだ。

Tom and Daisy were so rich they could do whatever they wanted. They even lived in France for a year. But they came back to America and just floated around here and there. Daisy said now they planned to stay in East Egg forever, but I didn't believe her. It seemed to me that Tom would continue to float around, searching for the same kind of excitement he had in his old football days.

One evening soon after I moved to West Egg, I went to visit Daisy and Tom. Their house was bigger and more cheerful than I expected. It looked over the bay and had a huge lawn that ran straight down to the beach. That evening, the sunset had turned all the front windows gold, and Tom was standing on the porch in his horse-riding clothes.

Tom had changed since his college days. Now he was a man of thirty, with a hard mouth and a proud manner. His clothes could not seem to contain the power of his large body. When he moved, you could see his muscles under his thin coat. It was a body that could do great harm. It was a cruel body. Tom made people feel small, and many of his classmates at college had disliked him. But for some reason, Tom had always liked me.

We talked on the porch before going into the house.

■float around ～のあたりを漂う　■here and there あちこち　■It seems to me that ～. 私には～のように思える。　■look over ～を見渡す　■turn ～ gold ～を金色に染める　■do harm 危害を加える　■make someone feel small 人を萎縮させる

トムとデイジーはありあまるほどのお金を持っていたから、好きなことは何でもできた。1年間フランスで暮らしていたこともある。でもまたアメリカに帰ってきて、あちらこちらを転々としていた。デイジーは今度こそイースト・エッグに落ち着くつもりだと言っていたが、僕は信じなかった。どうせトムが、かつてのフットボール時代と同じような興奮を求めて、これからも放浪をつづけるだろうと思っていた。

　ウェスト・エッグに移り住んで間もないある日の夕方、僕はデイジーとトムを訪ねた。家は思ったよりも大きくて明るい雰囲気だった。入り江を見下ろして建つ家から浜辺にむかって、広大な芝地がまっすぐ続いている。夕陽が家の正面の窓を黄金色に染めるなか、トムは乗馬服姿で玄関に立っていた。

　トムは大学時代とは変わっていた。今の彼は三十男で、その口もとは厳しく引き締まり、態度は偉そうだった。大きな肉体にみなぎる力が服に収まりきらないかのようだ。体を動かすたびに、薄い上着の下で筋肉が躍動するのが見てとれる。とてつもない危害をもたらしうる肉体。冷酷な肉体だ。トムは周りの人間を見下すところがあり、大学時代は彼を嫌う級友も少なからずいた。でもなぜかトムは、ずっと僕を気に入ってくれていた。

　家に入る前に、僕たちは玄関前で少し話をした。

"I've got a nice place here," Tom said. His eyes flashed around the grounds from here to there. Then he led me inside.

We went into the living room, where we met Daisy and another young lady seated on a couch. Both women were dressed in white and looked so pretty and light. Daisy laughed when she saw me. I laughed too.

"I'm so happy to see you!" said Daisy. "This is my friend Miss Baker."

The other young woman just nodded at me. She looked familiar, and I realized she was Jordan Baker, a famous professional golf player. Daisy looked up at me as if there were no other person in the world she would rather see. That was a way she had. She started to ask me questions in her lovely voice. It was a voice that you could follow like a strange piece of music. She had bright eyes and a bright mouth, and her face was both beautiful and sad.

I looked at Jordan again and suddenly I remembered that I had heard some story about her. It was something in the newspapers—something unpleasant—but it was a long time ago and I couldn't remember what it was.

"What are you doing these days, Nick?" Tom asked.

"I sell stocks," I said.

---

■flash 動（視線を）投げかける　■dressed in white 白い服を着て　■nod at ～に会釈する　■look familiar 見覚えがある　■as if まるで～のように　■would rather むしろ～したい

「なかなかいい家だろう」トムは言った。その目があたりをさまよって光った。しばらくして僕を中に入れてくれた。

居間に入ると、デイジーと若い女性が1人、カウチに座っていた。2人とも白いドレスを着ていて、軽やかで愛らしい。デイジーは僕を見ると笑い、僕も笑った。

「会えてとても嬉しいわ！」デイジーは言った。「こちらはお友達のミス・ベイカー」

若い女性はただ僕に頷くだけだった。どこか見覚えのある顔だと思ったら、あの有名なプロゴルファーのジョーダン・ベイカーだとわかった。デイジーは、この世で会いたかったのはあなただけ、というような目つきで僕を見上げた。それがデイジーのやり方だ。彼女はその可愛い声で質問をはじめた。ずっと耳を傾けていたい不思議な楽曲のような声色。瞳も口もとも輝きを帯び、その表情は美しくも悲しくも見えた。

ふたたびジョーダンに目をやると、ふと、前に何かの噂を聞いたことを思い出した。新聞で読んだ何か——それも良くないこと——だったと思うが、だいぶ昔のことなので、どんな内容か思い出せなかった。

「最近は何の仕事をしているんだ、ニック？」トムが聞いた。
「株を扱っている」僕は答えた。

"Don't you live in West Egg?" Jordan asked. "I know somebody who lives there. You must know him too, his name is Gatsby."

"Gatsby?" asked Daisy. "Who is Gatsby?"

Before I could reply that he was my neighbor, the dinner bell rang, and we all moved to the table that was set outside.

We sat down to eat and talked about this and that. Tom started to talk about a book he had read called "The Rise of the Colored Empires." He said it was important for us as white people to read it. He explained that science proved that the white race was the best and strongest race in the world, and we needed to watch out for other races that were trying to take over.

"We've got to beat those other races down," said Daisy. She winked at me, and I knew she was making fun of Tom.

Tom began to argue his point again when he was cut off by the loud ring of the telephone. The butler came out and whispered something into Tom's ear. Tom got up and went inside. After Tom had been gone a minute, Daisy stood up and went inside too. I did not think anything was the matter and started to say something to Jordan Baker. But she held up her hand and stopped me.

■this and that あれこれ、色々　■colored 形有色人種の　■watch out for 〜を警戒する　■take over（権力や土地などを）奪取する　■have got to 〜しなければならない　■beat 〜 down 〜を叩きのめす　■make fun of 〜をからかう　■cut off さえぎる、中断する　■hold up one's hand 手をあげる

「ウェスト・エッグに住んでいるの？」ジョーダンがたずねた。「あそこに住んでいる人を1人知ってるわ。あなたも知ってるでしょ、ギャツビーっていう人」

「ギャツビー？」デイジーが聞いた。「ギャツビーって？」

それは僕の隣人だ、と答える前に夕食を知らせるベルが鳴り、僕たちはそろって屋外に整えられたテーブルに移った。

席について食事をしながら、あれこれと話をした。そのうちトムは、読んだばかりの『有色帝国の興隆』という本について話しはじめた。白人として、僕たちも読んだ方がいいと言う。世界のあらゆる人種の中で白人が最も強く優れた人種であることは科学が証明しているとトムは言い、その座を奪おうとする他の人種に目を光らる必要があると語った。

「そんな他の人種は叩きつぶさなきゃ」とデイジーは言った。そして僕に目配せしてきたから、トムをからかっているんだとわかった。

トムがまた自説を繰り返そうとしたが、けたたましい電話のベルの音にさえぎられた。執事が外へ出てきて、何ごとかトムの耳にささやいた。トムは立ちあがり、部屋の中へ入っていった。トムがいなくなってしばらくすると、デイジーも席を立って部屋へ入った。僕は何かが起きているとは思わなくて、ジョーダン・ベイカーに話しかけようとした。ところが彼女はさっと手を上げて僕を止めた。

"Sh!" she said. "I want to hear what's going on." Then she leaned forward, listening to the faint voices coming from inside the house.

"Is something wrong?" I asked, surprised that Jordan didn't feel any shame in listening to other peoples' private conversations.

"You mean you don't know?" she asked. "I thought everybody knew."

"Knew what?"

"Tom has some woman in New York."

"Some woman?"

"I can't believe she would call him in the middle of dinner!" Jordan said. But Daisy and Tom returned to the table, and Jordan dropped the subject.

After dinner, we all sat in the living room again. Jordan read out loud to us from *The Saturday Evening Post*, and at ten o'clock, she went to bed. Daisy, Tom, and I were left together.

"She's a nice girl," said Tom.

"Yes. In fact, I think I shall make you marry her, Nick," said Daisy. "She's staying with us most of the summer and you'll see her often. I'll make sure you two fall in love and marry." She laughed her charming little laugh, and I knew she was not serious about any of it.

---

■what's going on 何が起こっているのか　■You mean ～? つまり～ってこと?　■in the middle of ～の最中に　■drop the subject 話題を打ち切る　■read out loud 声に出して読み上げる　■make someone do (人) に～させる　■I'll make sure ～. 必ず～します。

「しっ！」ジョーダンは言った。「どうなっているのか聞きたいの」彼女は身を乗り出し、かすかに漏れてくる声に耳をすませた。

「何かあったのかい？」ジョーダンが恥ずかしげもなく他人の話を盗み聞きしているのを見て僕は聞いた。

「何って、知らないの？」ジョーダンは言った。「みんな知ってると思ってた」
「知ってるって、何を？」
「トムにはニューヨークに女がいるの」
「女？」
「ディナーの最中に電話してくるなんて、信じられない女ね」ジョーダンは言った。でもデイジーとトムが戻ってきたので、その先は口を閉じた。

夕食後、僕たちは居間に戻って腰をおろした。ジョーダンは「サタデー・イブニング・ポスト」に載っていた話を大声で読み聞かせてくれ、午後10時になると寝室へ下がっていった。居間に残ったのはデイジーとトム、そして僕だけだ。

「彼女、素敵な女性だろ」とトムが言った。
「そうね。じっさい、あなたと結婚させたいくらいよ、ニック」とデイジーが言う。「彼女は夏の間ほとんどここにいるから、あなたともしょっちゅう会うことになる。きっと2人が恋に落ちて一緒になるようにしてあげるわ」デイジーが愛らしく小さく笑った。どれも本気では言っていない証拠だ。

"Nick, weren't you engaged to marry a girl out West?" asked Tom.

"No, that's not true. That's all rumors," I said.

Soon I got up to leave and headed home. As I drove back to West Egg, I felt confused and upset about what I had seen at Daisy and Tom's house. Tom was having an affair that everyone knew about. I thought Daisy should leave Tom forever. But Daisy did not seem to think that was necessary at all.

When I got home, I decided to sit outside for a while and look at the night sky. I was relaxing like this when I noticed a shadow about fifty feet away from me. A man stood with his hands in his pockets, looking across the bay. I realized it was probably my neighbor Gatsby. I was going to call out to him, but he suddenly stretched his arms out toward the bay, and it looked to me like his body was shaking a little. I looked toward the bay to see what he was looking at, but I only saw a single green light, like something at the end of a dock. When I looked once more for Gatsby, he was gone, and I was alone in the darkness.

---

■out 形遠く離れた　■drive back to 車で〜へ戻る　■have an affair 浮気をする
■not 〜 at all 全く〜ない　■like this こんなふうに　■call out 呼びかける
■stretch one's arms out 両腕を差し伸べる

「ニック、西部の女性と婚約したんじゃないのか？」トムが聞いた。

「いや、それは違う。まったくの噂だよ」

　間もなく僕は立ちあがり、暇を告げた。ウェスト・エッグの家まで車を走らせるあいだ、デイジーとトムの家で目にしたことで心が乱れ、動揺していた。おおっぴらに浮気をしているトムと、デイジーは縁を切るべきだ。でもデイジーは、そんな必要はまるでないと思っているみたいだった。

　家に着くと、しばらく外に座って夜空を見ようと思った。そうして気持ちを和らげていると、50フィートほど先に人影があるのに気づいた。男が1人、両手をポケットに入れて入り江を見渡している。隣人のギャツビーに違いないと思った。声をかけようとしたそのとき、彼は両腕を入り江に向けて伸ばした。その体がわずかに震えているように見えた。何を見ているのかと思って僕も入り江に目をやったが、見えるのは一点の緑色の光だけだった。桟橋の先につけられた灯りだろうか。ふたたびギャツビーの方を見たときには、もうその姿はなく、僕は暗闇に1人残されていた。

# 2

Between West Egg and New York is a sad-looking gray bit of land. It is a valley of dust, like some farm in a sad dream where dust grows like grain. Dust takes the shape of hills, houses, and even men who move like gray ghosts through the dust-filled air. Sometimes a line of train cars pulls up in the valley and comes to a slow stop. Then the gray ghost men pick up their shovels and dig into the train cars, stirring up a great cloud of even more gray dust.

But high above the gray land stands a great sight: the eyes of Doctor T. J. Eckleburg. The eyes of Doctor T. J. Eckleburg are blue and huge. Just the colored parts of the eyes are three feet high. The eyes are not a part of a face. They just stare out of a huge pair of yellow eye glasses. Some crazy eye doctor paid for this advertisement to be put there, in the land of dust, to increase his business. At some point he must have forgotten about it or moved away. But the eyes remained there, watching over the gray land with their yellow glasses.

■bit of わずかな〜　■pull up 乗り入れる　■come to a slow stop のろのろと停止する　■dig into 〜にずかずか立ち入る　■stir up 引き起こす　■stand a great sight ひどい風景を我慢する　■stare out of 〜から眺める　■at some point ある時点で　■watch over 〜を監視する

# 2

　ウェスト・エッグとニューヨークの間には、悲しげな灰色の一帯がある。そこは灰の谷間だ。灰が小麦のように育つ、悲しい夢の中の農場を思わせる。灰は丘をかたどり、家をかたどり、灰だらけの空気の中を灰色の亡霊のようにさまよう男たちの姿までかたどっている。ときおり、列車が谷間にやってきて、ゆっくりと停車する。すると灰色の亡霊たちはシャベルを手に取って車両に群がり、灰がいっそう舞い上がってあたり一面に立ち込める。

　しかし、その灰色の一帯にとんでもないものが立っている。T・J・エックルバーグ博士の両目だ。その目は青くて巨大だ。その目の着色部分だけでも3フィートの高さがある。目の他に顔の部分はない。2つの目だけが、巨大な黄色のメガネ越しに、じっとこちらを見つめている。どこかのおかしな眼医者が、患者を集めようとこの灰色の一帯に看板を掲げたのだろう。いつしか看板の存在を忘れたのか、あるいはどこかへ移り住んだかしたに違いない。でも両目は今もここに残って、黄色いメガネ越しに灰色の一帯を見張っている。

This unpleasant scene is where I met Tom's woman one day. Everyone knew that Tom was having an affair. Although I was curious about the woman, I had no desire to meet her. But one afternoon, as Tom and I drove into New York City for the day, Tom insisted on stopping. We were driving through the valley of dust when Tom said, "We're stopping here. I want you to meet my girl."

He pulled the car off the road and stopped it. We got out and I followed him across a dusty yard, under the huge staring eyes of Doctor Eckleburg. The only building in sight was a small block of yellow brick sitting on the edge of a little street. One of its three shops was a car repair shop. A sign in front read, "Repairs. George B. Wilson. Cars bought and sold." I followed Tom inside.

The inside of the shop was small and bare. The owner of the shop was clearly poor. The only car in the place was a broken old truck in a dark corner. Then the owner of the shop appeared from the office door. He was a thin man with light-colored hair. He looked very tired. He was wiping his dirty hands on a piece of cloth. When he saw Tom, a look of weak hope lit up in his eyes.

"Hello, Wilson," said Tom. He slapped the thin man cheerfully on the shoulder and asked, "How's business?"

■be curious about ～に興味がある　■have no desire to ～する気は毛頭ない
■pull the car off the road 道路から外れた場所に車を止める　■a sign reads 看板には～と書いてある　■a look of ～の表情

そんな不気味な土地で、僕はある日、トムの愛人に出くわした。トムに愛人がいることは誰もが知っていた。僕もその女に興味はあったが、会ってみたいとは少しも思わなかった。でもある日の午後、トムと僕は車でニューヨークへ向かったのだが、トムは途中で立ち寄りたいところがあると言い張った。灰の谷間を走っていたところでトムが言った。「ここで止まろう。僕の女に会ってくれ」

　トムは車を道の脇に寄せて止めた。僕は車を降り、トムのあとについて埃っぽい庭を歩いた。エックルバーグ博士の巨大な目が僕らを見下ろしていた。目に入る唯一の建物は、小さな道の端に積まれた黄色いレンガの小さな塊だけだった。建物には3軒の店が入っていて、そのうち1軒は自動車の修理工場だった。正面の看板に、「修理　ジョージ・B・ウィルソン　自動車販売・買取」とある。僕はトムについて中に入った。
　店は狭く、がらんとしていた。店主は金に困っているに違いなかった。そこにある唯一の車は、壊れた古いトラックで、隅の暗がりに止められていた。店主が事務所の戸口に現われた。やせた金髪の男で、ひどく疲れている様子だ。布きれで汚れた手を拭っている。トムに気づくと、その目にかすかな希望の光が浮かんだ。

「やあ、ウィルソン」トムは痩せた男の肩を威勢よく叩いて聞いた。「商売はどうだい？」

"I can't complain," Wilson said. It looked to me like there was plenty for Wilson to complain about.

"When are you going to sell me your car?" he asked Tom.

"Next week," replied Tom. "My man is working on it now."

"Seems like he works pretty slow," said Wilson. This angered Tom.

"No he doesn't," he replied coldly. "And if you feel that way about it, maybe I should sell it to somebody else."

Wilson looked scared.

"Oh, I don't mean to make trouble," said Wilson quickly. "I just mean—"

But his voice trailed off and Tom looked around the garage. We heard footsteps on the stairs, and in a moment the thick shape of a woman blocked the light coming from the office door. She was in her mid-thirties and was rather large, but she carried her extra weight pleasantly as some women can. Her face was not beautiful, but there was a visible air of life and excitement about her, as if her blood was always running hot.

She smiled slowly and walked past her husband toward Tom. She shook hands with Tom, looking straight into his eyes. She did not look at her husband as she said, "Go get some chairs, George, so these people can sit down."

■It looks to me like 〜. 私には〜のようにしか見えない。 ■my man うちの者、使用人 ■seem like 〜のように見える ■mean to 〜するつもりである ■trail off 次第に小さくなる ■block the light 光をさえぎる ■carry extra weight 余分な体重を有する ■air 图雰囲気 ■walk past 〜の脇をすり抜ける ■go get 〜を持ってくる

「文句は言えません」ウィルソンは答えた。僕には、文句が山ほどあるように見えた。

　「車はいつ売ってもらえますかね？」ウィルソンがトムに聞いた。

　「来週だな」トムが答える。「うちのものが今、手入れをしているところだ」

　「ずいぶん仕事の遅い方ですね」ウィルソンにそう言われ、トムはむっとしたらしい。

　「そんなことはない」と冷たく言い返した。「そんな風に思われているなら、他で売るべきかもしれないな」

　ウィルソンはたじろいだ。

　「いや、そんなつもりで言ったんじゃないんです」ウィルソンは慌てて言った。「ただ——」

　だがウィルソンの声はだんだん小さくなり、トムは店の中を見回した。階段を歩く足音が聞こえ、まもなく肉付きのいい女性のシルエットが、事務所の戸口から漏れる光をさえぎった。年の頃は30代半ばで、体つきは太めだが、余分な重みを魅力的にみせられる女の一人だった。美しい顔立ちではないものの、生き生きとして活気が感じられる。まるで、いつでも血が熱くたぎっているかのようだ。

　彼女はゆっくりと微笑み、夫の横を通り過ぎてトムの方へ歩み寄った。彼の手を握り、まっすぐ目を見つめる。そして夫の方を見ずに言った。「ジョージ、お客様が座れるように、椅子を持ってきてちょうだい」

"Oh, sure," said George. He hurried away to find some. When he was gone, the woman moved closer to Tom.

"I want to see you," Tom said. "Get on the next train."

"All right."

"I'll meet you by the newspaper stand on the lower level of the station," Tom said.

She nodded and moved away from him just as George entered the room with two chairs. Tom and I left. We drove to the nearest station and waited for her get on the train. A little child played in the gray dust on the side of the street.

"Terrible place, isn't it?" Tom said. He looked uneasily at Doctor Eckleburg.

"It's awful."

"It's good for her to get away from here," he said.

"What about her husband? Doesn't he say anything?"

"Wilson? He thinks she goes to see her sister in New York. He's so dumb he doesn't know he's alive."

■hurry away 急いで立ち去る ■get on 乗る ■stand 名 売り場 ■lower level 下の階 ■uneasily 副 不安げに ■get away from ～から抜け出す

「ああ、そうだな」ウィルソンは言って、急いで椅子を取りに行った。夫がいなくなると、彼女はトムに近寄った。
「君と会いたい」トムは言った。「次の列車に乗ってくれ」
「わかった」
「駅の下の階にある売店で会おう」トムが言った。

彼女がうなずいてトムから離れると、ちょうどウィルソンが椅子を2つ持って戻ってきた。トムと僕は店を後にした。最寄りの駅まで車で行き、彼女が電車に乗るのを待った。灰だらけの道端で、小さな子供が1人で遊んでいた。
「ひどいところだろう？」トムはそう言って、落ち着かなそうにエックルバーグ博士に目をやった。
「とんでもないところだ」
「ここから脱け出すのは彼女のためにいい」トムは言う。
「夫は？ 何も言わないのか？」
「ウィルソンか？ あいつは妻がニューヨークにいる妹に会いに行くんだと思っているよ。自分が生きているかどうかもわからないくらい間抜けなやつさ」

# 3

So it came to be that Tom, his girl, and I went together to New York. Well, sort of together. Tom and I rode in a different train car from his girl so that nobody would see us riding all together. At the train station in New York, we met his girl. Tom helped her down from the train. At a store in the station, she bought herself a magazine, some face cream, and a bottle of perfume. Once outside, she chose a new, purple-colored taxi for us to ride in. But as soon as we got into the taxi, she knocked on the driver's window to make him stop.

"I want to buy one of those dogs there," she said, pointing to a man standing on the street, selling puppies out of a basket. "A dog is nice to have in the apartment."

The driver stopped and Tom bought her a dog. Mrs. Wilson pet it happily while it sat in her lap.

When we drove up to Fifth Avenue, I finally said I had to go. I tried to stop the car and get out, but Tom wouldn't let me.

■come to 〜になってしまう  ■sort of 一種の〜、〜みたいな  ■so that 〜のために
■all together 一緒に  ■pet 動 なでる  ■drive up to（車で）〜まで走る

# 3

　そういうわけで、僕はトムと愛人と一緒にニューヨークへ行くことになった。厳密には「一緒」ではない。僕とトムは、彼女とは別の車両に乗ったからだ。3人一緒のところを知り合いに見られないようにするためだった。僕たちは、ニューヨークの駅に着いてから彼女のところへ行った。トムは列車を降りる愛人に手を貸してやった。彼女は駅の売店で、雑誌とフェイスクリーム、香水を買った。外へ出ると、車回しで紫色の新車のタクシーを選び、僕たちと乗り込んだ。ところが車が走り出して間もなく、運転手の後ろの仕切り窓をこんこんと叩いて、止まるように言った。

　「あそこの犬が1匹ほしいの」彼女はかごに入れた子犬を路上で売っている男を指差した。「あのアパートメントに犬が1匹いたら素敵でしょ」

　運転手はタクシーを止め、トムが犬を買ってやった。ウィルソン夫人は犬を膝に乗せて嬉しそうに撫でた。
　5番街まで来ると、ついに僕はもう失礼するよと切り出した。車を止めて降りようとしたが、トムが許してくれなかった。

"Myrtle will be hurt if you don't come up to see the apartment. Won't you Myrtle?" Tom said.

"Come on," she said to me. "I'll have my sister come over too, and lots of people say she's very beautiful."

"Well, I'd really like to—" I began, but nobody listened to me and the taxi drove on.

We arrived at the apartment on 158th Street. As we got out of the taxi, Mrs. Wilson looked around the street as if she owned it. She gathered her bags and went into the white apartment building with her nose high in the air.

"I'm going to invite the McKees to come over," she announced, as we went upstairs. "And of course, I'll call up my sister, too."

The apartment was on the top floor. It had a small living room, a small dining room, a small bedroom, and a bath. The living room was so crowded with big furniture that it was difficult to move around the room. There were several old magazines about movie stars and famous people on the table. The only picture in the room was a bad photo of a hen sitting on a rock. But I discovered that if you walked far enough away from the picture and looked at it again, the hen was actually a hat and the rock was actually the face of an old woman.

---

■come up(部屋に)上がる ■come over 訪ねてくる ■drive on 走り続ける
■with one's nose high in the air 鼻高々に ■call up 電話で呼び出す ■far enough away from ～からじゅうぶんに離れて

「アパートメントまで来てくれないと、マートルが悲しむ。そうだろう、マートル？」トムが言った。
「ねえ、来てよ」マートルが僕に言う。「私の妹も呼ぶから。すごい美人だってよく言われる子なの」
「いや、せっかくなんだけど──」僕は言いかけたが、誰も耳を貸してくれず、車は走り続けた。
　158丁目のアパートメントに到着した。タクシーから降りると、ウィルソン夫人は通りを自分の持ち物のように見まわした。それから荷物をまとめ、鼻を高く上げて白いアパートメントの建物に入っていった。

「マッキー夫妻も呼ぶことにするわ」彼女は上の階に向かうときに言った。「もちろん、妹も」
　部屋は建物の最上階にあった。小さな居間に、小さな食堂、小さな寝室、そして浴室がある。居間には大きな家具がひしめき、部屋の中を動くのも一苦労だった。テーブルには、映画スターや有名人の記事ばかりの古い雑誌が何冊か置かれていた。部屋に飾ってあるものといえば、岩の上に立つ鶏の、出来の悪い写真だけだった。ところが、写真からじゅうぶん離れてもう1度見てみると、鶏に見えたのは実は帽子で、岩は老女の顔だと気づいた。

Mrs. Wilson found a box and some milk for the dog. Tom brought out a bottle of whiskey from a locked closet.

I have only been drunk twice in my life. The second time was that afternoon, so everything that happened has a dreamy feel to it. At one point I went out to buy some cigarettes, and when I came back, Tom and Mrs. Wilson had disappeared. I sat waiting quietly in the living room until they appeared again a while later. By that time, I had already finished my first drink.

People began to arrive at the apartment. Catherine, Myrtle's sister, was a tall, thin girl of about thirty. She had a solid, sticky mass of red hair. The powder on her face made her skin milky white. Mr. McKee was a neighbor from downstairs. He was a small man who said he was a photographer. I found out later that it was him who had taken the picture of the old woman on the wall. The old woman was Myrtle's mother.

Although Mr. McKee's wife was pretty, she was loud and awful. She told me with pride that her husband had photographed her one-hundred and twenty-seven times since they had been married.

---

■bring out 取り出す　■drunk 形 酔っ払った　■have a dreamy feel to it 夢のようなぼんやりした感じがする　■make one's skin white 肌を白く見せる　■find out 発見する　■with pride 誇らしげに

ウィルソン夫人は寝床にする箱とミルクを犬に与えた。トムは鍵のかかった棚から、ウィスキーの瓶(びん)を取り出した。
　僕は人生で2度しか酔っぱらったことがない。その2度目がこの午後だった。だから、起きたことすべてに夢のような印象が残っている。途中で煙草を買いに出かけて戻ってくると、トムとウィルソン夫人の姿はなかった。居間に腰を下ろして大人しく待っていると、しばらくたって2人が帰ってきた。このときにはもう1杯目を飲み終えていた。

　アパートメントに人が集まりはじめた。マートルの妹キャサリンは、背が高くほっそりとした30歳くらいの女性だった。赤毛の髪は固くべとついた塊になっていて、顔色は白粉(おしろい)で乳白色になっている。マッキー氏は下の階の住人で、小柄な自称写真家だった。壁にかかった老女の写真を撮ったのはマッキー氏だと、僕は後になって知った。ちなみに老女はマートルの母親だという。

　マッキー夫人は美人だったが、騒がしくてひどかった。結婚して以来、マッキー氏に127回も写真を撮られていると自慢げに僕に語った。

Myrtle had changed her clothes a little earlier. Now she wore a fancy, cream-colored dress that made noises every time she moved. Along with her dress, her attitude seemed to change too. Her voice, her movements, and her laughter all took on an air of loud and rough pride. As she grew louder, the room seemed to grow smaller around her.

"I like your dress," Mrs. McKee said. "It's so pretty."

Myrtle brushed aside the praise right away.

"Oh, this? It's just a crazy old dress," she said, her nose held high in the air. "I only wear it when I don't care what I look like."

Tom yawned and stood up. "You McKees should have another drink," he said. "Myrtle, get some more ice for the drinks before everybody falls asleep."

"I told that servant boy to bring us some ice," said Myrtle. "These people! You have to stay on top of them all the time!" She looked at me and laughed as if I was agreeing with her every word. Then she picked up the dog and gave it a kiss. Then she got up and walked into the kitchen making extra noises with her dress, as if she had a dozen cooks waiting for her orders in there.

Her sister, Catherine, came and sat down next to me.

"Do you live down on Long Island too?" she asked.

"I live at West Egg," I replied.

---

■along with 〜と同調して　■take on（様相を）呈する、帯びる　■as A grows louder, B grows smaller Aがうるさくなるほど、Bが小さくなる　■brush aside 払いのける　■stay on top of 〜を完全に掌握する　■live down on 〜に住む

マートルは少し前に着替えていた。今はクリーム色の派手なドレスで、動くたびに布のこすれる音がする。ドレスとともに彼女の態度も変わってみえた。声色や身振り、笑い方まで、すべてが騒々しく荒っぽい尊大さをまとっていた。彼女がうるさくなるにつれ、部屋がどんどん縮んでいくようだった。

「いいわね、そのドレス」マッキー夫人が言う。「とっても素敵」
　マートルはその褒め言葉をすぐに払いのけた。
「これ？　ただの古い変なドレスよ」マートルは鼻を高く上げた。「身なりを気にしないときしか着ないの」
　トムはあくびをして立ちあがった。「マッキーさんも奥さんも、もう少し飲んだ方がいい」トムは言った。「マートル、みんなが寝てしまう前に、氷をもう少し持ってきてくれ」
「さっきボーイに氷を頼んだのよ」マートルは言った。「まったくあの連中は！　たえず見張ってなきゃいけないんだから！」彼女はこっちを見て、僕が彼女の言うことすべてに同意していると思っているみたいに笑った。そして犬を抱き上げてキスをした。それから立ち上がり、ドレスの音をひときわ大きくたててキッチンへ向かった。まるで、彼女を待つ十数人の料理人たちに命令を出しに行くみたいに。
　彼女の妹のキャサリンが僕の隣にやってきて腰を下ろした。
「あなたもロングアイランドにお住まいなの？」
「ウェスト・エッグに住んでいます」

"Really? I was at a party there about a month ago," she said, "at a man named Gatsby's. Do you know him?"

"I live next door to him."

"Well they say he's related to some German king, Kaiser Wilhelm or something," she said. "That's where all his money comes from."

Mr. McKee was speaking to Tom then, and I heard him saying that he would like to take more photos on Long Island.

"All I need is an introduction to get me started there," Mr. McKee was saying.

"Ask Myrtle," said Tom with a loud shout of laughter. "She'll write you a grand letter of introduction. You can photograph her husband and call it 'George Wilson Selling Gas,' or something." Tom roared with laughter.

Catherine leaned over and whispered to me, "Neither Tom nor Myrtle like the person they're married to."

"No?" I asked.

"No, they can't stand them. I think they should both get divorced and marry each other right away. But Tom's wife won't let him. She's Catholic and doesn't believe in divorce."

This was interesting because I knew Daisy wasn't Catholic. I was shocked at how deep Tom's lies went.

---

■relate to ～と関わりがある　■or something ～とか何とか　■would like to ～したい　■a letter of introduction 紹介状　■lean over 身を乗り出す　■can't stand ～に我慢ならない　■how deep his lies went 彼の嘘のなんと根深いことか

「本当に？ 1ヵ月くらい前にパーティーに行ったわ。ギャツビーという人の邸宅で。あの方をご存じ？」

「彼の隣に住んでいるんですよ」

「噂では、ドイツのヴィルヘルム皇帝か何かの親戚だとか」キャサリンは言った。「それで、あれだけのお金があるのね」

そのとき、マッキー氏がトムに、ロングアイランドでもっと写真を撮りたいと話しているのが聞こえた。

「紹介さえあれば、向こうで仕事が始められるんだが」マッキー氏が言った。

「マートルに頼むといい」トムはそう言って短く高笑いをした。「マートルが立派な紹介状を書いてくれるよ。彼女の夫の写真を撮れるようにね。作品の題は『ガソリンを売るジョージ・ウィルソン』でどうだろう」トムは大声で笑った。

キャサリンが僕の方に身を乗り出してささやいた。「トムもマートルも、結婚相手が好きじゃないのね」

「そうなのかい？」

「そうよ。相手に我慢ならないの。2人ともさっさと離婚して、一緒になればいいのに。でもトムの奥さまが許さないわね。カトリックだから、離婚なんて考えられないでしょう」

僕はデイジーがカトリックではないのを知っていたから、この話には驚いた。それに、トムがいかに念入りな嘘をついているかにも衝撃を受けた。

"Why did you ever marry George Wilson, Myrtle? You don't even like him, and nobody forced you to," Catherine said. Myrtle thought for a while.

"I married him because I thought he was a gentleman," she finally said. "But after I married him I knew it was a mistake. He had to borrow somebody's best suit to wear to our wedding. When I found that out, I cried all day long."

"She really ought to get away from him," Catherine said to me. "They've been living above that garage for eleven years and Tom is the first lover Myrtle has ever had."

The second bottle of whiskey got passed around. I wanted to get out and walk toward Central Park into the soft darkness of the night. But every time I tried to go, I would get caught up in some wild argument that pulled me back into my chair.

Suddenly, Myrtle was sitting very close to me and telling me about when she first met Tom.

"We were sitting in the same train car to New York," she said, her warm breath pouring over me. "He had on a nice suit and shoes. I couldn't keep my eyes off of him, and every time he looked at me I had to look away quickly. When we got off at the station, he pressed the front of his shirt to my arm and I told him I would have to call the police. But he knew I lied. I was so excited when I got into a taxi with him. All I kept thinking, over and over, was 'You can't live forever; you can't live forever.'"

■Why did you ever ~ ? そもそもなぜ~、一体どうして~ ■find ~ out ~に気付く ■all day long 一日中 ■ought to ~すべきである ■pass around 順に回す ■get caught up in ~に巻き込まれる ■can't keep one's eyes off of ~から目を離せない

「そもそも、どうしてジョージ・ウィルソンと結婚したの、マートル？ 好きでもなかったし、誰かに強いられたわけでもないのに」キャサリンが言うと、マートルはしばし考え込んだ。

「結婚したのは、あの人が紳士だと思ったからよ」ようやくマートルは言った。「でも、結婚してから間違いだと気づいた。あの人は自分の結婚式に、知り合いから晴れ着を借りなきゃならなかった。後でそれを知ったとき、一日中泣いたわ」

「姉は何としてもあの男と別れるべきね」キャサリンは僕に言った。「夫婦であの修理工場の上に11年も暮らしてるけど、マートルにとってトムこそが初めての恋人だわ」

2本目のウィスキーの瓶が僕たちの手から手へ回された。僕は早くここを抜けだして、セントラル・パークに向かって歩き、柔らかな夜の闇に包まれたかった。だが、帰ろうとするたびに白熱した議論に巻き込まれ、椅子に引き戻されるのだった。

いきなり、マートルが僕のすぐそばに座り、初めてトムに会ったときのことを話し出した。

「私たちはニューヨーク行きの列車の同じ車両に乗っていたの」マートルの生温かい息が僕に降りかかる。「上等なスーツを着て、いい靴を履いてた。もう目が離せなくて、彼がこっちを見るたび、慌てて目をそらしたわ。電車を降りると、彼が私の腕にシャツの胸元を押しつけてきたの。通報するわよって言ったんだけど、それが嘘だって彼はわかってたのね。彼とタクシーに乗りこんだときは、すっかり興奮してた。心の中で『人は永遠に生きられない、人は永遠に生きられない』ってひたすら繰り返したわ」

It was nine o'clock. Then suddenly it was ten o'clock. Mr. McKee was asleep on a chair. The dog was sitting on the table trying to see through the cigarette smoke. People disappeared, then appeared again. They made plans to go somewhere, then lost each other, searched for each other, and found each other a few feet away. Some time around midnight, Tom and Myrtle stood face to face, arguing. The argument was about whether Myrtle had any right to say Daisy's name.

"Daisy! Daisy! Daisy!" shouted Myrtle. "I'll say it whenever I want! Daisy! Dai—"

Suddenly Tom reached out and hit her with his open hand, breaking her nose.

Then there were bloody towels on the bathroom floor, and women's voices accusing Tom, and over it all, cries of pain. Mr. McKee woke up and looked at the scene around him. He took his hat and walked out the door. I followed him. Then I was lying half asleep on the cold lower level of Pennsylvania Station, waiting for the four o'clock train.

■lose each other はぐれる　■a few feet away すぐ横で　■face to face 面と向かい合って　■right 名権利　■reach out 手を伸ばす　■over ~ all ~の全体を通して

これが9時。次の瞬間には、10時になっていた。マッキー氏は座ったまま眠っていた。犬はテーブルの上に座り、煙草の煙の向こうを見すかそうとしている。人々は消えては現われ、どこかへ行こうと話し合い、それからお互いを見失い、探し合い、数フィート離れたところで見つけ合った。真夜中近く、トムとマートルは顔を突き合わせて立ち、言い合いをしていた。言い合いは、マートルにデイジーの名前を口にする権利があるかないかについてだった。

「デイジー！　デイジー！　デイジー！」マートルは叫んだ。「好きなときに言うわ！　デイジー！　デイ——」
　ふいにトムの腕が伸びて、マートルを平手打ちにした。彼女の鼻がつぶれた。
　やがて浴室の床には血だらけのタオルが散らばり、トムを責める女たちの声が響いて、そこに痛みの叫びがかぶさった。マッキー氏が目を覚まし、周りの光景を見回した。それから帽子を手にして扉の外へ出ていった。僕もあとに続いた。気づいたときには、寒々としたペンシルヴェニア駅の下のホームで半分寝そうになりながら横たわり、朝4時発の列車を待っていた。

# 覚えておきたい英語表現

> Tom and Daisy were so rich (that) they could do whatever they wanted. (p.18, 1行目)
> トムとデイジーはとても金持ちだったので、やりたいことをなんでもやれた。

【解説】so A that S + V「とてもAなので、SはVする」(注：S＝主語　V＝動詞)の構文です。that以下は、「主語＋動詞」のまとまり(節)が来ます。Aが原因・理由を表す形容詞・副詞が入り、that以下が結果を述べます。

本文中では、(that)が省略されています。話し言葉ではthatを省略することがありますが、その一例です。

soは「とても、非常に」という意味です。veryと同じように思えますが、veryは客観的であまり話し手の感情が入らない言い方で、soは主観的で話し手の感情が強く入る表現という違いがあります。

> It was so cold that we couldn't swim in the river.
> とても寒かったので私たちは川で泳げなかった。

このso ～ that構文は、作品中に何度も出てきますので覚えておくとよいでしょう。

＊p.36 3行目の "…so that nobody would see us riding all together." のso thatは「so that S will [can] V」＝「SがVする[できる]ように」という意味です。形が似ているので間違えないようにしましょう。

> It seemed to me that Tom would continue... (p.18, 4行目)
> 僕にはトムが……し続けるつもりであるように思えた。

【解説】It seems that { S + V } ＝「SがVするように思われる」の構文です。seemは「(主観的に)～のように思われる、らしい」という意味です。Itが主語の場合は

that節、人や物を主語にとるときはto不定詞の形をとることが多いです。to be 〜 の場合は省略されることもあります。

> It seems that he is tired.　または、He seems (to be) tired.
> 彼は疲れているようだ。

自分の目の前にいる人・物の外観や様子を述べる場合は、seemよりもlookやappearを用いることが多いです。

> My sister appears to know the man.
> 私の妹はその男を知っているようだ。

　本書にはseemを使った表現が頻出します。この小説が発表された1920年代初頭までは、アメリカ文学では、語り手は主人公(一人称)か、物語の出来事に関わらない第三者(三人称)が務めることが主流でした。語り手ニックは、主人公ギャツビーと深く関わる重要な登場人物です。そんな人物が物語の語り手を務めることは当時としては革新的だったのです。
　ニックの感覚を通して場面を描写する表現であるseemを目にするたびに、読者はあたかもニックその人になったかのような臨場感を感じつつ、自然と物語の世界に引き込まれていくのかもしれません。ぜひ、ニックとの一体感を感じながら物語を楽しんで欲しいと思います。

---

I like your dress.（p.42, 7行目）
あなたのドレスいいわね。

---

【解説】I like 〜は、相手の持ち物などを褒めるのに日常的に使える良い表現（しかも簡単！）ですが、これをサッと言える日本人は少ないのでは？　ネイティブらしい自然な表現ですからぜひ覚えてドンドン使って下さい。

| | |
|---|---|
| I like your new car! | お前の新しい車イイじゃん！ |
| I like your blue eyes. | あなたの青い目ステキね。 |
| I like your glasses. | かっこいいメガネしてるね。 |

# Part 2

# 4

Music came from my neighbor's house through the summer nights. In the afternoons, I would see his guests swimming in the ocean or lying on his beach. All day, his two motor-boats full of people would race across the blue waters, leaving long white trails behind them. On the weekends, his Rolls Royce became a bus that brought people to and from the city between nine in the morning and long past midnight. And on Mondays, eight servants and a gardener would work all day cleaning up the damage from the night before.

Every Friday, five wooden boxes of oranges and lemons came from a fruit shop in New York City. Every Monday, these same oranges and lemons left Gatsby's back door in a mountain of peels. There was a machine in the kitchen that could remove the juice from two hundred oranges in half an hour if somebody pressed a little button two hundred times.

■race across ～を渡って走る　■Rolls Royce ロールスロイス《高級車の名》　■to and from ～への送迎、往復　■long past ～をとっくに過ぎて　■back door 裏口　■remove A from B　BからAを取り出す

# 4

　夏のあいだずっと、夜は隣家から音楽が聞こえてきた。午後は、ギャツビーの客が海で泳いだり、邸宅の浜辺で休んだりする姿が見えた。彼の2隻のモーターボートは、一日中たくさんの人を乗せて青い海を疾走し、白く長い波の跡を引いた。週末は、ロールス・ロイスが街と邸宅を往復するバスとなり、朝の9時から真夜中をずっと過ぎるまで、客を送り迎えした。そして月曜日になると、8人の使用人と庭師が、一日がかりで前夜の被害をきれいに片づけるのだった。

　毎週金曜日には、木箱5箱分のオレンジとレモンがニューヨークの果物店から届いた。月曜日には、その同じオレンジとレモンが山盛りの皮になってギャツビー邸の裏口を出ていく。キッチンには、200回小さなボタンを押せば、200個のオレンジを30分でジュースにできる機械があった。

Every ten days or so, a group of hired help came with several hundred feet of white cloth and colored lights to make party tents in Gatsby's huge garden. Baked hams, chickens, salads, and fruits were arranged on long tables. There were so many different kinds of liquor in the bar that just the sight of them made you feel drunk.

By seven o'clock, the musicians would arrive—not some little five-piece band, but a full orchestra. By this time, the last swimmers would be back and dressing upstairs. There would be cars from New York parked all along the street, and already the halls and rooms would be full of bright colors and women with stylish haircuts. The bar would be busy, and waiters would be serving drinks in the garden. The air would come alive with voices and laughter. Women who never knew each other's names would greet each other warmly.

As the hour gets later and later, laughter spills out more easily. The lights burn brighter, and the groups of people change more quickly. They grow bigger with new arrivals and shrink as people float over to the next group. Confident girls move alone through groups of men, saying something clever and becoming the center of attention for a brief moment. Then they move on to the next group.

---

■or so ～かそこらで ■help 图従業員 ■just the sight of ～をちょっと見ただけで ■not A, but B AではなくB ■come alive 活気づく ■the hour gets late 遅い時間になる ■spill out こぼれる ■float over 流れていく ■move on 次に移る

およそ10日おきに、ギャツビーは大人数を雇って数百フィートの白い布と色つきの電球を持ちこませ、広大な庭にパーティー用テントをしつらえた。ベークト・ハム、チキン、サラダ、フルーツが長いテーブルに並べられた。バーにはあまりにたくさんの種類の酒が用意され、見ただけで酔いそうな光景だった。

　7時には、楽団がやってきた——といっても、5人編成の小さな楽団ではなく、本格的な管弦楽団だ。そしてこの頃になると、海で泳いでいた客も引き上げてきて、2階で着替えをした。通りにはニューヨークからきた車がずらりと並び、ホールや各部屋は鮮やかな色彩と流行りの髪型の女性たちで埋め尽くされた。バーは忙しくなり、ウェイターは庭で飲み物を出して回った。話し声と笑い声に空気が活気づく。互いの名前も知らない女たちが、会えて嬉しそうに挨拶をする。

　夜が深まるにつれ、笑い声が容易くこぼれるようになる。照明はまばゆさを増し、客の群れはより素早く形を変えていく。新しい客がやってきて膨らんだかと思うと、他の群れに人が移るにつれてしぼむ。自分に自信のある娘たちは、1人で男たちの群れに入っていき、気の利いたことを言っては束の間、注目の的になる。そしてまた別の群れへと去っていく。

At some point in the night, a girl grabs a drink out of thin air, drinks it down, and steps out onto the dance floor. The music changes to something a little faster, and she begins to dance all by herself. As more people join her, the party has really begun.

I believe that on the first night I went to Gatsby's house, I was one of the few people who were actually invited. Most people who came to the parties weren't really invited—they didn't need to be. They simply got into cars, made their way to Long Island, and showed up at Gatsby's door. They were never turned away. Some were introduced to Gatsby by somebody else who knew him, but some came and stayed the whole night without ever meeting Gatsby at all. And that seemed to be just fine.

Gatsby had actually sent his servant, dressed in a light-blue uniform, to my house to deliver an invitation. The card he handed to me said that Gatsby would be honored if I could attend his "little party" that night. It also said Gatsby had seen me several times before but never had a chance to meet me. It was signed "Jay Gatsby" in fancy writing.

■grab a drink 酒を1杯ひっかける　■out of thin air どこからともなく　■drink ~ down ~を飲み干す　■all by oneself 1人きりで　■show up 現れる　■turn away 追い払う　■would be honored if A could Aに~いただければ光栄だ

そんな夜のどこかの時点で、1人の娘がどこからともなくグラスをつかみ、一気に中身を飲み干すと、ダンスフロアに飛び出す。楽団は少しテンポの速い曲に演奏を変え、娘は1人で踊りだす。周りの客がどんどん加わり、パーティーが幕を開ける。

　はじめてギャツビー邸に行ったとき、僕は正式に招待された数少ない客の1人だったと思う。パーティー客のほとんどは招待などされていなかったし、その必要もなかった。彼らは単に車に乗って、ロングアイランドに向かい、ギャツビー邸の入口に現われただけだ。そこで追い返されることは決してなかった。ギャツビーを知っている人に紹介してもらう人もいれば、一晩中いてもギャツビーに1度も会わない人もいた。それで何の問題もないようだった。

　僕のところには、じっさいにギャツビーが淡い青色の制服姿の使用人をよこして、招待状を届けてくれた。招待状のカードには、ギャツビーがその夜に開く「ささやかなパーティー」に出席してくれたらこの上なく光栄だと記されていた。また、何度か僕を見かけたが挨拶をする機会がなかったことも書いてあった。最後には美しい書体で「ジェイ・ギャツビー」と署名されていた。

I put on my nice white suit and went over to his house a little after seven o'clock. I felt a little uncomfortable as I walked among groups of people I didn't know. I tried to find Gatsby as soon as I arrived to thank him for inviting me. But, try as I might, I could not find him anywhere. Feeling unhappy, I walked over to the bar and stayed there for a long time. It was the only place I could stay without looking so useless and alone.

I was on my way to getting very drunk when I saw Jordan Baker enter the garden. She stood on the steps leading from the house to the garden.

"Hello!" I shouted as I made my way toward her.

"I thought I'd see you here," she said. She rested her golden arm on mine, and we walked through the garden together. We sat down at a table where two girls dressed in yellow were sitting with three gentlemen.

"Do you come to these parties often?" Jordan asked the girl beside her.

"Sure," said the girl. "I like to come. I never care what I do here, so I always have a good time. When I was here last I tore my dress on a chair. Gatsby asked me my name and address and in one week I got a package with a new dress in it."

"Did you keep it?" asked Jordan.

---

■put on 着る ■go over to ～に出向いていく ■try as someone may どんなにがんばっても ■on one's way to ～しつつある ■steps 图 階段 ■rest one's arm on 腕を～の上に置く ■Sure. もちろん。ええ。

僕はきちんとした白いスーツを着て、7時少し過ぎにギャツビーの家に行った。見知らぬ人たちの中を歩くのはちょっと居心地が悪かった。招待してくれた礼を言おうと、着いてすぐにギャツビーを探したが、どこにも見当たらなかった。しかたなくバーに向かい、長い間そこにいた。手持ちぶさたで寂しそうに見えない唯一の場所だったからだ。


　ひどく酔っ払いかけていたところで、庭へ出ていくジョーダン・ベイカーの姿が見えた。邸宅から庭につづく階段の上に彼女は立っていた。

　「やあ！」僕は大声で呼びかけ、彼女の方に行った。
　「ここで会える気がしてたわ」ジョーダンは言った。そして黄金色の腕を僕の腕にまわし、一緒に庭を歩いた。僕たちは、黄色いドレスを着た2人の娘と、3人の紳士が座っているテーブルについた。

　「あなたはここのパーティーへよく来るの？」ジョーダンは隣の娘に聞いた。
　「ええ。ここに来るのは好きよ」娘は答えた。「ここでは何をしても気にしなくていいから楽しく過ごせる。前に来たとき、ドレスを椅子に引っかけて破ってしまったの。そうしたらギャツビーに名前と住所を聞かれて、1週間後には新しいドレスが届いたのよ」
　「それ、受け取ったの？」ジョーダンがたずねた。

"Sure I did," said the girl. "I was going to wear it tonight, but it was a little too big and had to be fixed. It was gas blue with purple beads. Two hundred and sixty-five dollars."

"There's something strange about a man who will do a thing like that," said the other girl. "He doesn't want trouble with anybody. Somebody told me—" the two girls and Jordan leaned in toward each other and spoke in quiet voices.

"Somebody told me they thought he killed a man once." The statement got us all excited. The three men leaned forward to hear.

"No, I heard he was a German spy during the war," said the other girl. One of the men nodded in agreement.

"I heard that from a man who knew all about him, and even grew up with him in Germany," the man said.

"Oh, no," said the first girl, "that can't be, because he was in the American army during the war." Now we all believed her instead of the other man, and she added, "Just look at him sometimes when he thinks nobody is looking. I bet he killed a man."

We all turned to look for Gatsby, but of course he was nowhere to be found.

■lean in toward 〜の方に体を寄せる　■get 〜 excited 〜を興奮させる　■instead of 〜の代わりに　■Just look at 〜. ちょっと〜を見てみて。　■I bet 〜. 〜に違いないと思う。〜だと賭けてもいい。

「もちろん。今夜着るつもりだったけど、ちょっと大きいから直さないといけなくて。くすんだ青い生地に紫のビーズがついたドレスで、お値段は265ドルですって」
「そういうことする男の人って、なんだか奇妙ね」もう1人の娘が言った。「誰とも面倒を起こしたくないみたいで。誰かに聞いたんだけど——」
娘2人とジョーダンは身を寄せ合い、ひそひそ声で話しはじめた。

「誰かに聞いたんだけど、あの人は人を殺したことがあるらしいの」その発言でみんなが愕然とした。3人の紳士も身を乗り出して聞き耳を立てた。
「まさか。戦争中はドイツのスパイだったって私は聞いたわ」もう1人の娘が言った。紳士の1人が頷いた。
「その話、彼のことなら何でも知ってるという男から聞いたよ。ドイツで一緒に育ったらしい」紳士が言った。
「それはないわ」最初の娘が言った。「それはありえない。だって戦争中はアメリカ軍の兵士だったんだもの」今度はみんな、紳士の話ではなく彼女の話を信じた。娘は付け加えた。「誰にも見られていないと思っているときのあの人を見てごらんなさい。私、絶対に人を殺してると思うわ」
僕たちはいっせいに振り返ってギャツビーを探したが、やっぱりどこにもいなかった。

# 5

After supper, Jordan and I tried to find Gatsby. First, we went to the bar, but he was not there. Then we went to the top of the stairs to look down onto the garden, but she couldn't see him. We wandered into a very large, old-fashioned library, but he wasn't there either.

When we went back outside, people were dancing in the garden. By midnight, everyone was drunk and laughing. A few famous singers at the party had sang some songs, the champagne was being served in glasses that were the size of bowls, and the moon had risen higher. Jordan was still with me. We sat at a table with a man of about my age and a loud young girl who laughed at everything. After all the champagne, I was feeling very happy.

During a pause in all the talking and laughing, the man looked at me and said politely, "Your face is familiar to me. Were you in the Third Division during the war?"

"Why, yes, I was."

---

■wander into ～に迷い込む、立ち入る　■a man of about one's age 同年代くらいの男　■laugh at ～を笑う　■be familiar to 覚えがある、馴染みがある

# 5

　食事の後、ジョーダンと2人でギャツビーを探した。まずバーに行ったが、そこにはいなくて、階段のいちばん上から庭を見渡しても、ジョーダンには見つけられなかった。僕たちはとてつもなく広い古風な図書室にさまよい込んだが、そこにも彼はいなかった。

　ふたたび外へ出ると、客たちは庭でダンスをしていた。真夜中になると、誰もが酔って笑っていた。有名な歌手が何人か登場して歌を披露し、シャンパンがボウルのような大きなグラスで振る舞われ、月はさらに高く昇った。ジョーダンはまだ僕と一緒にいた。僕たちは、僕と同年代の男と、何に対しても笑う騒がしい娘のいるテーブルについた。シャンパンをたくさん飲んで、僕はすっかり上機嫌だった。

　あれこれ談笑していると、その男が僕の顔を見て礼儀正しくこう言った。「あなたのお顔に見覚えがあります。戦時中、第3師団にいらっしゃいませんでしたか？」
　「ええ、確かにいましたが」

"I was in the army until June of 1918. I knew I had seen you somewhere before."

We talked for a moment about some little villages in France. Then he told me he had just bought a new motor-boat and invited me to take it out on the water with him the next morning.

"Sure, what time?" I said.

"Any time you like."

I was just about to ask the man his name when Jordan turned around and said to me, "Are you having a good time now?"

"Much better now," I said, and turned back to the man.

"This is an unusual party for me," I said. "I haven't even seen the host. I live over there—" I waved my hand toward my house across the lawn, "and this man Gatsby sent his servant over to invite me."

For a moment he looked at me as if he didn't understand.

"I'm Gatsby," he said suddenly.

"What! Oh, I beg your pardon."

---

■take 〜 out on the water 〜を水に浮かべる ■be just about to まさに〜するところだ ■turn around 振り返る ■turn back 向き直る ■send 〜 over 〜を送ってよこす ■I beg your pardon. 失礼しました。

「私は1918年の6月まで軍にいました。きっとどこかでお見かけしたんだと思います」
　僕たちはしばし、フランスの小さな村々の話をした。それから彼が、新しくモーターボートを買ったので翌朝一緒に乗りませんかと提案した。

　「いいですね。何時にしましょう？」僕は言った。
　「あなたのお好きな時間でいいですよ」
　彼に名前を聞こうとしたとき、ジョーダンがこっちを振り返って僕に言った。「どう、楽しんでる？」
　「ずっと気分がいいよ」僕は答えて、男に向きなおった。
　「こういうパーティーは珍しいですね。僕はまだ、ここの主人にもお目にかかってないんです。僕はあそこに住んでいるんですが——」僕は芝生の向こうの自分の家を手で示した。「ここのギャツビーという方が、使いをよこして招待してくれたんです」
　一瞬、男はわけがわからないという風に僕を見た。
　「私がギャツビーです」彼はだしぬけに言った。
　「何ですって！　ああ、これは失礼しました」

"I thought you knew, old sport. I'm afraid I'm not a very good host," said Gatsby. Then he gave me a smile that was full of understanding and warmth. It was one of those precious smiles that seemed to reassure you about everything you've ever done in your life. It saw you as you hoped others would see you, it believed in you as you would like to believe in yourself, it respected who you were. But just as I saw all this, the smile disappeared, and I was just looking at a fashionable young man.

Just then, a servant hurried over to Gatsby and said somebody from Chicago was calling on the phone. Gatsby bowed to all of us and excused himself. Before he left, he turned to me and said, "If you want anything just ask for it, old sport. Excuse me. I will join you again later."

When he was gone I turned to Jordan. He was not anything like I expected. For some reason I had thought Gatsby would be a rather fat man in middle age.

"Who is he?" I asked. "Do you know?"

"He's just a man named Gatsby," said Jordan.

"Yes, I know, but where is he from, I mean? And what does he do?"

"Oh, now *you're* curious about it," she answered with a smile. "Well, he told me once that he went to Oxford for college. But I don't believe it."

■old sport きみ、親友《友人への呼称、大仰な響きを持つ》 ■I'm afraid 残念ながら〜、恐縮ですが〜 ■believe in 〜を信頼する ■hurry over to 〜へ慌てて行く ■excuse oneself 席を外す

「もうご存じだと思っていたんですよ、きみ。至らぬ主人ですみません」ギャツビーはそう言って、思いやりと親しみに満ちた笑顔を僕に向けた。それは、人生でしてきたことをすべて受け止めてくれるような、掛け値なしの笑顔だった。この人は自分が望むように自分を見てくれる、自分が信じたいように自分を信じてくれる、ありのままの自分を尊重してくれる、そう思わせる笑顔だ。だがそう思った次の瞬間には、笑顔は消え、目の前にはただ洗練された若い男性だけがいた。

そのとき、執事が急いでやってきて、ギャツビーにシカゴから電話が入っていますと告げた。ギャツビーはみんなに失礼しますと会釈をした。そして立ち去る前に僕の方を向いて言った。「もしご用がありましたら、何でも言ってくださいね、きみ。では失礼します。またあとでお会いしましょう」

ギャツビーが行ってしまうと、僕はジョーダンの方を振り向いた。ギャツビーは僕の予想とまるで違っていた。なぜか、太った中年男性を思い浮かべていたのだ。

「彼は誰なんだ？　きみは知ってる？」

「彼はただギャツビーという名前の人よ」ジョーダンは言った。

「それはわかってるけど、どこの出身とか、何の仕事をしてるか、とか」

「今度はあなたも気になりだしたのね」ジョーダンは笑顔で言った。「前に、オックスフォード大学に通ってたって本人に聞いたわ。私は信じないけど」

"Why not?"

"I don't know. I just don't think he went there," she said. "Anyway, he gives large parties. I like large parties."

Later in the night, as I was listening to the music and watching different people dance, my eyes fell on Gatsby, standing alone on the grand steps. He looked from one group to another, watching everyone. He was handsome, and his short hair looked like it was cut perfectly every day. I could see nothing evil or bad in him, as others seemed to. I wondered if the fact that he did not drink separated him from his guests. The more his guests drank and laughed, the more correct and wise Gatsby seemed to me.

When a slow song started, girls put their heads on men's shoulders, and couples danced slowly. But no girl put her head on Gatsby's shoulder. No one danced with him.

"I beg your pardon." One of Gatsby's servants was standing next to us and speaking to Jordan.

"Are you Miss Baker?" he asked. "Mr. Gatsby would like to speak to you alone."

"With me?" Jordan asked with surprise.

"Yes, Miss."

■from one to another 次から次へと ■wonder if 〜ではないかと思う ■separate A from B AをBから分かつ、切り離す ■put one's head on someone's shoulder 頭を人の肩にもたせかける

「どうして？」

「どうしてかしら。ただ、あそこへは行ってない気がするの」ジョーダンは言った。「とにかく、彼は大きなパーティーを開いてくれるし、私は大きなパーティーが好き」

その後、演奏を聴きながら他の客が踊っているのを見ていると、大階段の上に1人で立っているギャツビーの姿が目に入った。ギャツビーは客の集団を1組ずつ眺めていた。ハンサムな顔立ちで、短い髪は毎日手入れされているようだった。周りの人が言うような邪悪さを、僕はまるで感じなかった。彼が周りの客と別世界にいるように見えるのは、酒を飲まないからだろうか、と僕は思った。客たちが酔って陽気になればなるほど、ギャツビーが理路整然として賢く見えるのだ。

テンポの遅い曲が始まると、娘たちは男たちの肩に頭をもたせかけ、カップルはゆっくりと踊った。だが、ギャツビーの肩に頭をもたせかける娘も、ギャツビーと踊る娘もいなかった。

「失礼いたします」ギャツビーの執事が僕たちのところへやってきて、ジョーダンに声をかけた。

「ベイカー様でいらっしゃいますか？ ギャツビー氏がお2人でお話をなさりたいそうです」

「私と？」ジョーダンは驚いて聞き返した。

「ええ、そうです」

She got up slowly, looking at me with large, surprised eyes. She followed the man into the house. Then I was alone, and it was almost two o'clock in the morning. I decided to move inside. A large room was full of people. One of the girls in yellow was playing the piano, and singing beside her was a tall, red-haired young lady from a famous theater group. She had had a lot of champagne, and during her song she had decided that everything was very, very sad. She was not only singing, but weeping too. Her tears rolled down her cheeks, making black trails down her face.

"She had a fight with a man who says he's her husband," explained a girl standing near me.

I looked around. Most of the remaining women were now having fights with their husbands. In the hall were two couples. The two men were not drunk at all, and the two women were angry. The women spoke to each other in raised voices.

"Whenever he sees I'm having a good time, he wants to go home," one said.

"I never heard of anything so selfish in my life," the other said.

"We're always the first ones to leave."

"So are we."

"Well, we're one of the last to leave tonight," said one of the men in a small voice. "The orchestra left half an hour ago."

■the girl in yellow 黄色い服の女の子　■not only A, but B　Aのみならず B も
■tears roll down one's cheek 涙が頬を伝い落ちる　■well 間 ええと、その

ジョーダンはゆっくり立ち上がり、目を丸くして僕の方を見た。そして執事について家の中に入っていった。僕は1人残され、時間は午前2時になろうとしていた。僕も中に入ることにした。広々とした部屋は人で溢れかえっていた。黄色いドレスの娘の1人がピアノを弾き、その横で有名な合唱団に所属している背の高い赤毛の若い女性が歌っていた。彼女はシャンパンを飲みすぎていて、歌っているうちに、この世のすべてがひどく悲しいと思い込んでしまったらしい。ただ歌うだけでなく、すすり泣いてもいた。涙が頬を流れおち、黒い跡を残した。

「彼女、自分が夫だと名乗る男とけんかしたの」と僕の隣にいた娘が教えてくれた。
　僕は周りを見回した。今やパーティーに残っている女たちのほとんどが夫とけんかをしていた。ホールには2組の夫婦がいた。男たちは2人とも素面だったが、女たちは激昂し、互いに声を張り上げてしゃべっていた。

「私が楽しんでいるのを見ると、あの人はすぐ帰りたがるの」1人が言う。
「そんな自分勝手な話、聞いたことないわ」もう1人が言う。
「いつだって私たちが最初に帰る客なんだから」
「私たちだってそう」
「いや、今夜は最後に帰る客だよ」男の1人がぽそりと言った。「楽団は30分前に引き上げてるんだ」

After a bit more arguing, the night ended for both couples with the men picking up their wives and carrying them out the door. The women kicked, but they all disappeared into the night.

As I waited for my hat in the hall, the door of the library opened and Jordan and Gatsby came out together. He was saying some last words to her, but he saw some of his guests leaving and started to say goodbye.

Jordan came over to me and shook my hand.

"I've just heard the most unbelievable thing," she whispered. "How long were we in there?"

"About an hour," I told her.

"It was . . . unbelievable," she repeated. "But I swore I wouldn't tell anyone about it." She yawned. She seemed tired. "Please come and see me some time . . . Goodbye." She joined the party of people she had come with and walked out the door.

I stepped toward Gatsby to say goodbye and to apologize for not knowing him in the garden earlier.

"Don't worry about it, old sport," said Gatsby, shaking my hand. "Don't give it another thought. And don't forget we're going out in my boat tomorrow morning."

Then one of his servants said behind Gatsby's shoulder, "Somebody in Philadelphia is calling you on the phone, sir."

"All right, tell them I'll be there in a minute," Gatsby replied. Then to me he said, "Good night, old sport. Good night."

■pick up 抱き上げる、抱え上げる ■carry 〜 out 〜を運び出す ■wait for my hat（預けていたのを受け取るため）帽子を待つ ■come over to 〜にやって来る ■join a party 一行に加わる ■Don't give it another thought. もう気にしないで。

もう少しばかり言い合いが続いたあと、2組の男女の夜は、妻が夫に外へ担ぎ出される格好で終わった。女たちは足をばたつかせたが、やがて夜の闇に消えていった。

　ホールで預けた帽子が出てくるのを待っていると、図書室の扉が開いてジョーダンとギャツビーが一緒に出てきた。ギャツビーは最後に何かを彼女に伝えていたが、客が何人か帰るのに気づくと、別れの挨拶をしにいった。

　ジョーダンが僕のところへやってきて握手をした。

　「たった今、とても信じられないことを聞いたの」彼女は囁いた。「私たち、どのくらいあそこにいたかしら？」

　「1時間くらいかな」僕は答えた。

　「ほんと……信じられない」彼女は繰り返した。「でもね、絶対に人には言えないことなの」彼女はあくびをした。くたびれているようだった。「また、私に会いに来てね……さようなら」彼女はパーティーに連れ立ってきた人々と合流し、帰っていった。

　僕はギャツビーに歩み寄り、別れの挨拶をして、庭で彼に気づかなかったことを詫びた。

　「きみ、どうかお気づかいなく」ギャツビーは僕の手を握って言った。「もう気になさらないで。それより、明日の朝、ボートに乗る約束を忘れないでくださいよ」

　そのとき、執事がギャツビーの背後にやってきた。「フィラデルフィアからお電話が入っています」

　「わかった。すぐ出ると伝えてくれ」ギャツビーは執事に告げた。それから僕に向かって言った。「お休みなさい、きみ。お休みなさい」

# 6

After reading over everything I have written, I realize that it sounds like parties were all that I cared about. That's not true. Actually, I was very busy that summer, and what took up most of my time was work. In the early morning, I hurried down the streets of New York City to the business district. I would work all day and go to lunch with other men my age. I usually had dinner at the Yale Club, and then I went upstairs to the library and studied stocks for about an hour. After that, if it was a nice night, I would go for a walk down Madison Avenue.

I began to like New York. It felt fast and busy and always full of people. There was adventure everywhere. But sometimes, later at night as I walked through the streets, I felt a sinking feeling of loneliness. And I could tell others felt it too — sometimes I saw other young working men walking all alone to dinner. I knew they felt as lonely as me.

■read over 読み返す　■sound like 〜のような印象を受ける　■care about 関心を持つ　■take up 消費する　■hurry down 駆け下りる　■men of one's age 同世代の男たち

# 6

　ここまで書いたものを読み返してみると、僕がパーティーにばかり気を取られていたように読めてしまうことに気づいた。それは事実ではない。じっさい、あの夏はとても忙しくて、ほとんどの時間を仕事に割いていた。朝早い時間に、ニューヨークの通りをビジネス街に向かって急ぎ足で歩いた。そこで一日中仕事をして、同じ年頃の男たちと昼食に出た。夕食はたいていイェール・クラブで済ませ、食後は上階の図書室で1時間ほど証券の勉強をした。その後、天気の良い夜ならば、マディソン・アヴェニューを散歩した。

　僕はニューヨークという街が好きになりはじめていた。動きが早くて忙しく、いつも人で溢れている。あらゆる場所に冒険がある。でもときどき、夜遅くに通りを歩いていると、沈むような寂しさを感じた。同じ気持ちを周りの人も感じているのがわかった——ときおり、働いている若者が1人きりの夕食に向かう姿を見かけた。僕と同じように孤独だったと思う。

I didn't hear from Jordan Baker for a while. But in the middle of summer, we connected again. At first I felt lucky to be able to go places with her, because she was a famous golfer and everyone knew her name. But then this feeling turned into something more. It was not love, but I felt a tender curiosity toward her. The bored, proud look on her face seemed to hide something, and I wondered about it. One day, I found out what it was.

We were at a party at somebody's house. Jordan borrowed somebody's car and left it out in the rain with the top down, and then she lied about it. Suddenly I remembered the unpleasant story about Jordan that I could not remember the first night I met her at Daisy's house. Jordan had cheated in her first golf tournament. It was such a big deal that the story made it into the newspapers. People said that she had moved her ball from a bad spot on the course. But then the witnesses took back their statements, and everybody forgot the whole thing.

Jordan was a dishonest person, and that's what she was hiding from the world. But I didn't care. And sooner or later, I forgot about it.

The evening we were coming home from the house party where Jordan had lied about the car, she drove me home. She was a bad driver, and she almost hit a person on the street.

■hear from ～から連絡をもらう ■go places あちこち遊び歩く ■turn into ～に変化する ■wonder about ～を怪しむ ■leave ～ out ～を放置する ■with a top down （オープンカーの）屋根を下げたままで ■take back 撤回する ■hide from the world 世間の目をそらす

しばらくジョーダン・ベイカーからの便りはなかった。けれど夏の盛りに僕たちはまた会うようになった。最初は、彼女と色々なところへ行けるのが嬉しかった。何といっても、彼女は誰もが知る有名なゴルファーだったからだ。ところが次第に、それ以上の気持ちに変わっていった。恋というのではないけれど、愛着のまじった好奇心を抱くようになったのだ。退屈そうで尊大な顔つきは何かを隠しているようで、それが何なのか気になった。ある日、僕はその答えを知ることになる。

　誰かが開いたハウス・パーティーでのことだった。ジョーダンは、知り合いに借りた車の屋根を下ろしたまま雨の中に置いてきてしまい、そのことで嘘をついた。ふいに、デイジーの家で最初に会った時に思い出せなかった噂、新聞に載った良くない話が何だったかを思い出した。彼女が初めて出場したゴルフ・トーナメントでずるをしたという話だ。当時はものすごい騒ぎになり、新聞沙汰になった。自分のボールを悪い位置から動かしたという話だったが、その後、指摘した人物が発言を撤回し、みんなこのことは忘れてしまった。

　ジョーダンは不正直な人間だ。それこそ彼女が世界に隠している姿だ。でも僕は気にしなかったし、そのうち忘れてしまった。

　ジョーダンが車のことで嘘をついたその夜、ハウス・パーティーからの帰りは彼女の車に乗せてもらった。彼女は運転が下手で、危うく人を轢きそうになるほどだった。

"You're a terrible driver," I said to her. "You should either be more careful or not drive at all."

"I am careful," she said.

"No, you're not."

"Well, other people are," she said lightly.

"What does that have to do with it?"

"They will keep out of my way," she said. "It takes two people to make an accident."

"What if you met somebody as careless as yourself?"

"I hope I never will," she answered. "I don't like careless people. That's why I like you."

It was one of the first tender things Jordan had ever said to me, and for a moment, I thought I loved her. But then I remembered that there was a certain girl back home in the Midwest to whom I was still writing letters every week. And although I knew I shouldn't, I was signing those letters "Love, Nick." I knew I had to break it off with this girl before I was free.

Everyone has some goodness in them in one way or another. For myself, I believe my goodness comes from the fact that I am one of the few honest people that I have ever known.

---

■either A or B AかそれともB　■What does that have to do with it? それとこれとがどう関係あるの？　■keep out of one's way 道をあける、よける　■a girl back home 故郷の彼女　■break 〜 off 〜を解消する　■in one way or another 何らかの形で

「きみの運転はひどいな」僕は言った。「もっと注意するか、運転はすっぱりやめるかした方がいいよ」

「私は注意してる」

「いや、してない」

「でも、周りの人がしてるから」彼女はあっけらかんと言った。

「だから何だい？」

「私のことをよけてくれるでしょ。片方が注意していれば、事故は起きない」

「もしきみと同じくらい不注意な人に出くわしたら？」

「そうならないように祈る」彼女は答えた。「私、不注意な人って嫌い。だからあなたが好きなの」

これはジョーダンが初めて僕にかけた優しい言葉の1つだった。一瞬、彼女のことを愛しいと思った。でも、自分には中西部の故郷にある女性がいるのを思い出した。僕はこの当時も、毎週その女性に手紙を書いていた。そうすべきではないとは知りつつも、手紙の最後にはいつも「愛をこめて、ニック」と署名していた。自由になるためには、彼女との関係を解消しないといけないのはわかっていた。

誰にでも、その人なりの良さがある。僕の場合は、自分が知るかぎり数少ない正直者の1人だということが、それに当たると思う。

# 覚えておきたい英語表現

> Feeling unhappy, I walked over to the bar... (p.60, 5行目)
> 落ち込んだ気持ちになったので、僕はバーの方へ歩いて行き……

【解説】分詞構文 Ving 〜 , S+V'「VなのでSがV'する」の構文です。分詞とは動詞の変化した形で、現在分詞と過去分詞の2つがあります。分詞で始まる語句全体が、副詞の働きをするものを「分詞構文」といいます。意味は「〜なので(理由)」、「〜した時に(時)」、「〜しながら(同時)」などが主ですが、これにあてはめにくい文例も多数あるので、コンマの前後で2つ別々の文に分けて、意味がつながるように訳するとよいでしょう。

Being tired, I stayed at home all day.
疲れていたので、一日中家にいたよ。

Seeing Mary, I was reminded of my daughter.
メアリーを見た時に(見たので)、私は娘のことを思い出した。

Thinking about the deadline, I'd better help you.
締め切りのことを考えたら、僕は君の手伝いをするべきだろうね。

＊p.148 15行目〜16行目にも現在分詞を用いた分詞構文がありますので、気に留めておいて下さい。過去分詞を用いた分詞構文は、「〜された」と受け身で訳します。

Seen by many people, she turned red.
多くの人に見られたので彼女は赤くなった。

> I bet he killed a man. (p.62, 下から3行目)
> 彼きっと人を殺してるわよ。

【解説】betは、賭けをするという意味です。I bet ～で、「～だということに賭けてもいい」＝「きっと～だと断言する」という意味になります。

> I bet he can't do that.
> 彼はそんなことできっこないよ。

＊場面によっては、疑いを示す使い方もあります。

> "I was thinking about you!" "Yeah, I bet."
> 「君のことを考えていたのさ！」「さあ、どうだか」

> The more his guests drank and laughed, the more correct and wise Gatsby seemed to me. (p.70, 10行目)
> 客が酔って笑うほど、ギャツビーの謹直さが増してくるように思えた。

【解説】The 比較級～、the 比較級……「～すればするほど、ますます……」の構文です。文頭にThe比較級を見たらこのパターンを思い出して下さい。慣れておくと便利な表現です。

> The deeper you dive, the higher the water pressure becomes.
> 深く潜れば潜るほど、水圧が高くなる。

> The more I stare you, the more I love you.
> 君を見つめれば見つめるほど、ますます君が恋しくなる。

> ... I am one of the few honest people that I have ever known.
> （p.80, 下から2行目）
>
> ……僕が知ってる範囲では、僕は数少ない誠実な人間の1人だ。

【解説】[the 最上級]＋[現在完了形（経験用法）]「今まで〜したなかで、一番……だ」の構文。最上級は、比較表現の1つで、"the 〜 est" か "the most 〜" で表現します。現在完了形（経験用法）と相性がよいので、セットで用いられる場合があります。覚えておくと良いでしょう。

> This is the most beautiful sunset that I have ever seen.
> これは今まで見た中で一番美しい夕焼けだ。

　ちなみに本書を最後まで読むと、「僕は数少ない誠実な人間の1人だ」と、ニックが自分を評する理由に得心がいくことと思います。

# Part 3

# 7

That summer, the most rich and powerful people in the country came to Gatsby's house. Even some people from far away—some as far as Europe—came to his house. It was a very, very long list of people.

One morning in late July, at around nine o'clock, Gatsby's beautiful car pulled up to my door and gave a burst of sound from its horn. It was the first time he had ever come to visit me, although I had gone to two of his parties, ridden on his boat, and often used his beach.

"Good morning, old sport. You're having lunch with me today," said Gatsby. He saw me admiring his car.

"It's pretty, isn't it, old sport?" he said, and he jumped out of the car. "Haven't you ever seen it before?"

I had seen it. Everybody had seen it. It was a rich cream color, with light purple leather seats. I got into the car and off we drove to the city.

---

■far away 遠く離れて　■pull up （車を）止める　■give a burst of sound 突然大きな音を出す　■pretty 形 魅力的な、きれいな　■get into the car and off we drove 車に乗り込んで私たちは出発した

# 7

　その夏、ギャツビー邸には国内屈指の財力と権力を持つ人々が訪れた。遥か遠くの地から──はるばるヨーロッパから──やってくる客もいた。訪問客のリストは果てしなく伸びていった。

　7月下旬のある朝、9時頃、ギャツビーの美しい車が僕の家の前に止まりクラクションを鳴らした。彼が訪ねてくるのは初めてのことだった。これまで僕は、彼のパーティーに2度ほど行き、ボートに乗せてもらい、たびたびビーチを使わせてもらっていた。

「おはよう、きみ。今日は昼食を一緒に取る約束でしたね」ギャツビーは言った。そして、僕が彼の車に見とれているのに気づいた。
「きれいな車でしょう、きみ」ギャツビーは勢いよく車から降りた。「まだ見たことはありませんでしたか？」
　見たことはあった。誰だって見たことがある。車体は深みのあるクリーム色で、シートは薄紫色の革張りだ。僕が車に乗り込むと、2人でニューヨークへ出発した。

I had talked to Gatsby about six times in the past month, and I was disappointed to find out that he didn't really have much to say. So my first idea of him as a man of some importance quickly disappeared. Instead, I thought of him simply as a rich man with a big house next door.

But then we had this strange little ride into the city. We hadn't even left West Egg before Gatsby started acting strangely. He didn't finish his sentences and he started slapping his knee as if he were thinking hard about something.

"Look here, old sport," he finally said, "what's your opinion of me?"

I was a little surprised and couldn't answer right away. But Gatsby kept talking.

"I'm going to tell you something about my life," he said. "I don't want you to get the wrong idea of me. There are all these false stories of me floating around. I'll tell you the truth: I am the son of some wealthy people in the Midwest. They're all dead now. I was raised in America but educated at Oxford, because all my family have been educated there for many years. It's a family tradition."

He looked at me quickly, and I knew then why Jordan Baker didn't believe him. It was the way he rushed through some of the details, as if they bothered him. Now I didn't believe him either.

■not have much to say 話題に乏しい　■think of ～を評価する　■finish one's sentence 話を終える　■Look here. ねえ。ちょっといいですか。　■right away すぐに　■float around 出回る　■rush through 急いで終わらせる

このひと月のあいだに、ギャツビーとは6回ほど話す機会があったが、彼が大した話をしないので僕はがっかりしていた。ただ者ではないという第一印象は、瞬く間に消えてしまった。そのかわり、単に隣の豪邸に住んでいる金持ちの男、という風に考えるようになった。

　しかしそんなときに、この奇妙なドライブをすることになった。まだウェスト・エッグを抜けないうちに、ギャツビーは奇妙な振る舞いをはじめた。何かを言いかけてはやめ、必死に考え事をしているみたいに膝を叩いた。
「ねえ、きみ」ついにギャツビーは言った。「私のことをどう思いますか？」
　僕は少し驚いて、すぐに答えられなかった。でもギャツビーは話しつづけた。
「私の生い立ちについて話しておきたいんです。きみには誤解してほしくありません。でたらめな噂話が出回っていますからね。きみには真実を話しますよ。私は、中西部の裕福な家に生まれました。親族はもうみんな死んでいます。育ったのはアメリカですが、大学はオックスフォードへ行きました。先祖代々むこうで教育を受けてきましたからね。いわば家族の伝統というやつです」

　ギャツビーはさっと僕を見た。このとき、どうしてジョーダン・ベイカーが彼を信用しないのかがわかった。それは彼が詳細を飛ばして話すせいだ。まるで細かい話が煩わしいとでも言うように。これで僕もギャツビーを信用しなくなった。

"What part of the Midwest?" I asked.

"San Francisco," he said.

"I see."

"My family died and left me all their money." He looked serious. To me, at least this statement seemed true.

"For a while, I lived like a king, just traveling and spending money and living only for myself. I was trying to forget something very sad that had happened to me. But then came the war, old sport. I tried very hard to die, but for some reason I was never killed. Instead, I ended up leading a group of soldiers far into enemy territory and making the Germans in that area surrender. I was given awards from every government in the Allied forces. Even little Montenegro down in the Adriatic Sea!"

He reached into his pocket and pulled out a piece of metal attached to a bit of ribbon. He put it in my hand.

"That's the one from Montenegro," he said.

I was shocked. The thing looked real!

"Turn it," he said. I did, and I read his name on the backside of the military award.

"Here's another thing I always carry. It reminds me of my Oxford days." He gave me a photograph, where a bunch of young men were relaxing on the grass in front of a school that looked like Oxford. Gatsby, a little younger, was in the crowd.

---

■I see. なるほど。分かりました。　■but then しかしその一方で　■came the war 戦争が始まった《倒置法》　■try hard to ～に尽力する　■end up 結局～となる　■make ～ surrender ～を降参させる　■reach into ～に手を突っ込む　■a bunch of 大勢の～

「中西部のどのあたり？」僕は聞いた。

「サンフランシスコです」彼は答えた。

「なるほど」

「家族が死んで、全財産を私に残してくれたんです」彼の顔は真剣だった。少なくともこの言葉は、真実であるように思えた。

「しばらくの間、王様みたいな暮らしをしていました。あちこちを旅して、贅沢をし、自分のためだけに生きてきました。自分の身に起きたどうしようもなく悲しい出来事を忘れようとしていたんです。そこへ戦争が起きたんですよ、きみ。私はどうにか死のうと努力しました。でも、なぜか殺されなかった。そのかわり、兵士の一団を敵地深くまで率いたときに、その地域にいたドイツ軍を降伏させたんです。おかげであらゆる同盟国から勲章を授与されました。アドリア海に面したあの小さなモンテネグロからも！」

ギャツビーはポケットからリボンの付いた金属片をひとつ取り出し、僕の手にのせた。

「それはモンテネグロから授与されたものです」

僕は衝撃を受けた。いかにも本物らしかったのだ！

「裏返してみて」言われたとおりにすると、勲章の裏に彼の名前が刻されていた。

「もう1つ持ち歩いているものがあります。オックスフォード時代の思い出です」ギャツビーは1枚の写真を差し出した。何人もの若い男たちが、オックスフォードらしき校舎の前の芝生でくつろいでいる写真だ。今より少し若いギャツビーが、その中にいた。

So it was all true! This was evidence of his past.

"I'm going to make a big request of you today," he said, "so I wanted you to know something about me. You see, I surround myself with people I don't know so I can forget the sad thing that happened to me. But you'll hear about it this afternoon. I found out that you're taking Miss Baker to tea today. I asked her to tell you about it."

I had no idea what he was talking about, and I was a little upset with him. Why did he have to ruin my tea with Jordan? I didn't ask her to go to tea with me just to talk about Gatsby. But he wouldn't say another word, and we continued to drive to the city.

At noon, Gatsby and I walked into a restaurant on Forty-second Street. Gatsby introduced me to a man who was waiting for us in the restaurant.

"Mr. Carraway, this is my friend Mr. Wolfsheim," Gatsby said.

A small, flat-nosed man raised his large head and looked at me with his tiny eyes. He shook my hand. Gatsby led us both to a table and we sat down.

"I like this place," Mr. Wolfsheim said, "but I like across the street better."

"It's too hot there," Gatsby said, looking at his menu.

"Hot and small, yes," said Mr. Wolfsheim, "but full of memories."

■make a request of ～に頼みごとをする　■surround oneself with ～に囲まれる
■have no idea まったく分からない　■be upset with ～が頭にくる

ということは、すべて真実なのか！　ここに過去の証拠があるのだから。
　「今日はきみに大きな頼みごとがあります。だから、私のことをいくらか知ってもらいたかったんです。私が知らない人達に囲まれて暮らしているのは、あの悲しい出来事を忘れるためなんです。でも、きみは午後にその出来事について知るでしょう。今日、ベイカーさんとお茶の約束があると聞いたので、彼女から話してくれるように頼んでおきました」

　僕はギャツビーが何を言っているのか理解できず、おまけに少し腹も立った。どうしてジョーダンとのお茶の時間を台無しにするんだろう？　彼女をお茶に誘ったのは、ギャツビーの話をするためではないのに。でもギャツビーはそれ以上何も言わず、街に向けて車を走らせつづけた。
　お昼に、42丁目のレストランに入った。店で待っていた男性をギャツビーは僕に紹介した。

　「キャラウェイさん、こちらは友人のウルフシャイム氏です」
　小柄で平べったい鼻をした男は、大きな頭を上げ、小さな目で僕を見た。僕たちは握手をした。ギャツビーに案内されて、3人でテーブルについた。
　「なかなかいい店だ。でも私は、通りの向こうの店の方が好きだが」ウルフシャイム氏は言った。
　「あそこは暑すぎます」ギャツビーはメニューに目を落としたまま言った。
　「暑くて狭い、その通りだ。でも思い出が詰まっている」

"What place is that?" I asked.

"The old Metropole," said Mr. Wolfsheim. "It's filled with faces dead and gone. Filled with friends now gone forever. I can't forget for as long as I live the night they shot Rosy Rosenthal there. There were six of us at the table, and Rosy drank a lot all evening. It was almost morning when the waiter came up with a strange look and said, 'There's somebody who wants to speak with you outside.' Rosy said 'All right,' and began to get up from his chair. But I pulled him back down and said, 'Let them come in here if they want you, but don't you move out of this room!'" Mr. Wolfsheim paused.

"Did he go?" I asked.

"Sure he went," Mr. Wolfsheim said. "He turned around at the door and said, 'Don't let that waiter take away my coffee!' Then he went out to the street, and they shot him three times in his stomach and drove away."

I remembered reading the news about it. Rosy Rosenthal was a gangster who was famous around New York. He was known for gambling and selling liquor. "Four men were sentenced to death in the trial," I said.

"Five," Mr. Wolfsheim said. Then he looked at me in an interested way. "So I understand you're looking for a business connection," he said.

■old 形かの、昔なじみの ■Metropole 名メトロポール《ホテルの名前》 ■dead and gone とっくに死んでいる ■as long as someone live 生きている限り ■pull ~ back down ~を下(椅子)へ引き戻す ■take away 片付ける ■sentence to death 死刑判決を下す

「どこの店です？」僕はたずねた。

「懐かしの〈メトロポール〉ですよ」ウルフシャイム氏が言った。「今は亡き顔ぶれで溢れている場所です。永遠にこの世を去った仲間たちの思い出がね。あの店でロージー・ローゼンタールが撃たれた夜のことは一生忘れない。テーブルには私たち6人が座っていてね。ロージーは一晩中飲んでいた。もう夜が明ける頃、ウェイターが妙な顔をしてやってきて、ロージーに言ったんだ。『あなたと外で話したいという方がいらしてます』と。ロージーは『わかった』と言って席を立とうとした。でも私は引き留めて言った。『用があるなら向こうに来させればいい。だがお前はここから出ていくな！』」ウルフシャイム氏はそこで間をおいた。

「で、行ったんですか？」僕は聞いた。

「もちろん行ったさ。ロージーはドアのところで振り向いてこう言ったよ。『ウェイターに俺のコーヒーを下げさせるな！』 そして通りへ出た。そこで腹を3発撃たれて、あいつらは車で走り去った」

この事件について新聞で読んだのを思い出した。ロージー・ローゼンタールはニューヨーク周辺で有名なギャングで、賭博や酒の密売で名を馳せていた。「4人が死刑判決を受けましたよね」僕は言った。

「5人だ」ウルフシャイム氏は訂正した。それから興味深そうに僕を見た。「それで、仕事上の人脈を探しているんだったね」

Gatsby jumped in. "Oh, no," he said. "This isn't the man."

"No?" Mr. Wolfsheim looked disappointed.

"No, this is just a friend," said Gatsby. "I told you we would talk about that some other time."

"I beg your pardon, I thought you were another man," said Mr. Wolfsheim.

Our lunch arrived, and we began to eat.

"Look here, old sport," said Gatsby to me, "I'm afraid I made you rather angry in the car earlier."

"I don't know what this is all about, and I don't like mysteries," I said. "Why can't you just tell me what you want? Why does it have to come through Miss Baker?"

"Oh, don't worry, old sport. It's nothing bad," said Gatsby. Suddenly he looked at his watch, jumped up, and walked away from the table.

"He has to use the telephone," said Mr. Wolfsheim. He had finished his lunch and was now drinking his coffee. "Gatsby's a fine fellow, isn't he? He's handsome and a perfect gentleman."

"Yes," I said.

"He's an Oxford man," said Mr. Wolfsheim. "It's one of the most famous colleges in the world."

"Have you known Gatsby for a long time?" I asked.

---

■jump in 割り込む　■what this is all about これが一体どういうことなのか
■come through（情報などが）伝わる

「違いますよ」ギャツビーが割って入った。「それはこの彼じゃありません」

「違うのか？」ウルフシャイム氏はがっかりした様子だった。

「違います。彼はただの友達です。あの件はまた後で話そうと言ったでしょう」

「失礼しました。別の方と勘違いしまして」ウルフシャイム氏は詫びた。

食事がテーブルに並んで、僕たちは食べはじめた。

「ねえ、きみ」ギャツビーが僕に言った。「さっきは車の中で怒らせてしまったようで申し訳ありません」

「何が何だかわからない。謎めいたことは好きじゃないんだ」僕は言った。「何かあるなら自分で言ったらいいじゃないか。どうしてベイカーさんを通す必要があるんだい？」

「まあ心配しないでくれますか、きみ。決して悪いことじゃないんです」ギャツビーは言った。そして急に腕時計を見ると、急いで席を立ってテーブルを離れた。

「電話をしなきゃならないようだ」ウルフシャイム氏が言った。彼はもう食事を終えて、コーヒーを飲んでいた。「ギャツビーはいいやつだろう？　ハンサムで完璧な紳士だよ」

「そうですね」僕は言った。

「あいつはオックスフォードの出身だ。世界一有名な大学の1つだよ」

「ギャツビーとは古くからの付き合いなんですか？」

"Several years," he answered. "I met him right after the war." He paused and said, "I see you're looking at my shirt buttons."

I wasn't looking at them, but now that he directed my attention to them I did. They were made of strange white shapes. They looked like bone.

"The finest examples of human teeth," said Mr. Wolfsheim.

"Oh!" I said in shock.

Just then Gatsby returned and Wolfsheim got up to leave.

"Well, I should be going now," he said. "I have enjoyed my lunch, but I am much older than either of you, and I should be going." Mr. Wolfsheim shook our hands and walked away.

"He's quite a character," said Gatsby, watching his friend walk out of the restaurant.

"Who is he? An actor?"

"No, he's a gambler," said Gatsby. "He's the man who arranged for the Chicago White Sox to lose the World Series in 1919."

I was shocked. "That's the man who set up the World Series? That was a terrible scandal! How did he do that?"

"He just saw the opportunity," said Gatsby.

"Why isn't he in prison?"

"They can't get him, old sport. He's a very smart man."

■right after 〜直後の　■I see 〜. 〜だとお見受けします。　■direct someone's attention to 〜に目を向けさせる　■be made of 〜でできている　■quite a character かなりの変わり者　■arrange for 〜の手はずを整える　■set up 仕組む

「数年かな。戦争が終わってすぐに知り合ったんだ」ウルフシャイム氏は間をおいて言った。「きみは私のシャツのボタンを見ているようだが」
　見てなどいなかった。でも、そう言われて視線がそこに移った。白くて不思議な形をしたボタンだった。骨みたいだ。

「実によくできた人の歯の標本だよ」ウルフシャイム氏は言った。
「えっ！」僕は驚いて言った。
　そこへギャツビーが戻ってきて、ウルフシャイム氏は席を立った。
「私はそろそろ行かなくては」彼は言った。「楽しい時間を過ごせたよ。私はきみたちよりだいぶ年寄りだから、そろそろ失礼しないとな」ウルフシャイム氏は僕たちと握手をして、帰っていった。
「なかなかいない人です」ギャツビーはレストランを出ていく友人の背中を見て言った。
「何者なんだい？　俳優？」
「いえ、賭博師です。1919年のワールドシリーズで、シカゴ・ホワイト・ソックスが負けるように八百長を仕組んだ男ですよ」
　僕は唖然とした。「彼がワールドシリーズで八百長を？　とんでもない騒ぎだったじゃないか。いったいどうやって？」
「ただ、タイミングをつかんだのです」ギャツビーは言った。
「どうして刑務所行きにならないんだ？」
「捕まえられないからですよ、きみ。とても賢い男だから」

# 8

That afternoon, I had tea with Jordan Baker as planned. She sat very straight in her chair at the Plaza Hotel and began to tell her story.

"One October day in 1917," she said, "I was walking on the street outside of Daisy Fay's house. Daisy was eighteen years old at the time—two years older than me. She was the most popular girl in our town, Louisville. She dressed in white and had a little white car. All day long the telephone rang in her house and excited young army officers would ask to see her.

"I saw her that morning, sitting in her car with a handsome young army officer. I had never seen him before. They were talking with such passion to each other that she didn't even see me until I was five feet away.

"'Hello, Jordan!' she called out to me. 'Please come here.'

---

■sit straight 背筋を伸ばして座る　■army officer 陸軍士官　■with such passion すごく情熱的に

# 8

　午後は予定通りに、プラザホテルでジョーダンとお茶を飲んだ。ジョーダンは背筋をまっすぐ伸ばして座り、話をはじめた。

　「1917年の10月のある日、私は道を歩いていて、デイジー・フェイの家の前を通りかかったの。あのときデイジーは18歳で、私のふたつ年上。ルイヴィルの町では一番人気の女の子だった。白い服を着て、小さな白い車に乗っていた。家には朝から晩まで、胸をときめかせた若い将校たちから会いたいって電話がかかってきてたみたい。

　その日の午前中に見かけたとき、デイジーは白い車の中で若くてハンサムな将校と一緒にいたの。その男の人のことは、それまで見たことがなかった。2人は情熱的に語り合っていて、私が近づくまで気づかなかったくらい。
　『あら、ジョーダン！　ちょっとこっちへ来て』ってデイジーは言ったわ。

"I was happy she was speaking to me because of all the older girls, I admired her most. She asked if I was going to the Red Cross that evening to make bandages. I told her I was. She asked if I would mind telling them that she couldn't come that day. The officer looked at Daisy while she was speaking in a way that every girl hopes to be looked at some time. His name was Jay Gatsby. I never saw him again until four years later. Even after I met him on Long Island, I didn't realize it was the same man.

"That was 1917. By the next year I had become more popular and I was playing in golf tournaments so I didn't see Daisy often. There were some wild stories around town about her. Some said her mother found her one night packing her bags and saying she was going to New York to say goodbye to some soldier who was going to war. Her mother stopped her, but Daisy didn't speak to her family for a long time after that.

"By the next autumn she was lively again—as lively as ever. In February she seemed to be engaged to a man from New Orleans, but in June she married Tom Buchanan of Chicago. It was the biggest wedding Louisville had ever seen. He came down with a hundred people in four private cars. The day before the wedding he gave her a string of pearls that was worth three hundred thousand dollars.

---

■ask if ～かどうか尋ねる  ■mind 動 ～を嫌がる、気にする  ■in a way that ～というやり方で  ■wild story いいかげんな話  ■pack one's bag (荷物をまとめて) 出て行く  ■as ～ as ever 従来どおりに～  ■string of 数珠つなぎの～

デイジーが話しかけてくれて嬉しかった。だって、年上のお姉さんたちの中で、彼女が一番の憧れだったから。今夜は包帯を作りに赤十字へ行くの？ と聞かれて、ええと答えた。すると、自分は今日は行けないとみんなに伝えてほしい、って言われたの。デイジーが話しているあいだ、例の将校さんはじっと彼女を見てた。女の子ならみんないつかはそんな風に見つめられたいっていう目でね。その人の名前が、ジェイ・ギャツビーよ。それきり4年後に再会するまで彼を見かけることはなかった。ロングアイランドで会ってからも、あの時の将校さんだとは気づかなかった。

　これが1917年の話。次の年には私もだんだんお声がかかるようになったし、ゴルフのトーナメントに出たりもしていたから、デイジーに会うことも減ったの。町では、彼女に関する大きな噂がいくつか出回ったわ。ある夜、荷造りしているところを母親に見つかって、出兵するある兵士に別れを告げにニューヨークへ行くと言ったらしい、とかね。デイジーは母親に引き留められて、それから長いあいだ家族と口を聞かなかったみたい。

　秋が来る頃には、デイジーはまた元気になっていた——以前のようにね。2月にはニュー・オーリンズ出身の男と婚約したと言われてたけど、6月に結婚した相手はシカゴ出身のトム・ブキャナンだった。ルイヴィル史上、最も盛大な結婚式だったわ。トムは列車の車両を4台借りきって100人もの列席者を引き連れてきた。そして式の前日には、デイジーに30万ドルもする真珠のネックレスを贈ったの。

"I was invited to her wedding. I went into her room half an hour before the wedding dinner and found Daisy lying on her bed, completely drunk. She had a bottle in one hand and a letter in the other.

"'What's the matter?' I asked.

"'Here, dearest,' she said and handed me a waste basket. In it was the string of pearls. 'Go and tell them Daisy changed her mind!' She began to cry and cry. I ran downstairs and got another woman to help. Together, we locked the door and put Daisy in a cold bath. She wouldn't let go of her letter. She only agreed to put it on the soap dish when we showed her that it was falling apart in the water.

"But she didn't say anything else. The next day, she married Tom Buchanan, and they left for a three-month trip to the South Seas.

"I saw them in Santa Barbara when they returned from their trip. Daisy seemed to be completely in love with Tom. She would sit with his head in her lap and run her fingers through his hair for hours. A week after I left Santa Barbara, I heard Tom got into a car accident. There was a woman in the car, too. She also got into the newspapers because her arm was broken. She was a maid at a hotel in Santa Barbara.

---

■What's the matter? どうしたの？　■dearest 名いとしい人《親しみを込めた呼びかけ》　■do and do ～しまくる　■let go of ～から手をはなす　■fall apart バラバラになる　■run ～ through … ～を…に通す、くぐらせる　■get into ～に巻き込まれる

私も結婚式に招待された。披露宴の30分くらい前に部屋を訪ねたら、デイジーはベッドで横になっていて、完全に酔っ払っていた。一方の手にはお酒の瓶を、もう一方の手には手紙を握っていた。

　『いったいどうしたの？』って聞いたわ。
　『はい、これ』デイジーはそう言ってくずかごを差し出した。中には、あの真珠のネックレスが入っていた。『みんなに言ってきてよ、デイジーは気が変わったって！』デイジーは泣きだして止まらなくなった。私は階段を駆け下りて、1人の女性に助けを求めたわ。一緒に、部屋の鍵を締めて、デイジーを冷たいお風呂に入れた。デイジーは手紙を放そうとしなかった。水に濡れて崩れてしまうのに気づいて、ようやく石鹸皿に置くことを許してくれた。
　でも、デイジーは他に何も言わなかった。次の日、彼女はトム・ブキャナンと結婚して、南太平洋へ3ヵ月の旅に出発した。

　旅行から戻ってきた2人に、サンタ・バーバラで会ったわ。デイジーはトムにすっかり夢中みたいだった。トムに膝枕をしたまま何時間も髪を撫でてあげたりしてね。私がサンタ・バーバラを発って1週間後、トムが自動車事故に遭ったと知ったわ。彼の車には女も1人乗っていたの。女が腕を骨折したから新聞に名前が出ちゃったんだけど、それがなんとサンタ・バーバラのホテルのメイドだったの。

"The next April, they went to France for a year. Then they lived in Chicago. Daisy was very popular in Chicago. But they decided to move to Long Island, and now here they are.

"About six weeks ago, Daisy heard the name Gatsby for the first time in years. It was when I asked you — do you remember? — if you knew Gatsby in West Egg. After you left that night, Daisy came to my room and asked, 'Who is Gatsby?' When I described him, she said in the strangest voice that it must be the man she used to know. Then I realized he must have been the young officer in her white car."

By the time Jordan finished telling me all of this, we had left the Plaza Hotel and were driving through Central Park.

"Gatsby bought that house so Daisy would be just across the bay," said Jordan.

I remembered the first night I saw Gatsby. He had stood at the edge of his lawn and stretched his arms out across the bay.

"He wants to know if you'll invite Daisy to your house some afternoon and then let him come over," she said.

I couldn't believe it. The man had waited five years just so he could "come over" some afternoon in the hopes of running into Daisy.

"Did I have to know all this before he could ask me such a little thing?" I asked.

■for the first time in years 何年かぶりに初めて　■used to 以前〜していた　■just so one can まさに〜するためだけに　■come over 訪ねてくる　■run into 〜と偶然に出くわす

次の年の4月から1年間、トムとデイジーはフランスに行っていた。その後しばらくシカゴに住んだ。デイジーはシカゴでみんなに好かれていたけど、2人はロングアイランドに移り住むことにした。で、今に至るというわけ。

　6週間くらい前、デイジーは何年かぶりにギャツビーの名前を耳にしたの。それがあのときよ、覚えてる？　私があなたに、ウェスト・エッグのギャツビーを知ってるかって聞いたとき。あの夜、あなたが帰った後、デイジーが私の部屋にやってきて聞いたわ。「ギャツビーって、どんな人？」って。説明してあげたら、彼女は別人のような声色で、昔知ってた男に違いないって言ったの。それで私も気がついた。ギャツビーは、あの白い車にいた若い将校なんだって」

　ジョーダンが全てを話し終える頃には、僕たちはプラザホテルを後にして、セントラル・パークで馬車に揺られていた。

　「ギャツビーがあの家を買ったのは、入り江のすぐ向こうにデイジーがいるからなの」ジョーダンは言った。

　僕はギャツビーを初めて見た夜のことを思い出した。彼は芝生の縁に立ち、入り江に向かって両腕を伸ばしていた。

　「それでギャツビーは、あなたが近いうちの午後にデイジーを家に招待して、そこへ自分も顔を出させてくれるかどうか、知りたいそうよ」

　とても信じられなかった。5年も待っておいて、いつかの午後にただ「顔を出して」デイジーに出くわすのが願いだなんて。

　「そんな小さな頼みごとのために、今までの話を全部聞く必要があったのかな？」僕は聞いた。

"He's afraid," said Jordan. "He's waited so long. He thought you might not like it."

"Why didn't he ask you to arrange a meeting?"

"He wants her to see his house," she explained. "And your house is right next door."

"Oh!"

"I think he sort of expected her to wander into one of his parties some night," said Jordan. "But she never did. Then he began asking people if they knew her, and I was the first one he found. It was that night that he called me into his library to speak to me. But when I said you were a friend of Tom's, he seemed to not want to go through with it at all."

It was getting dark, and the ride through Central Park felt nice. Suddenly I wasn't thinking of Gatsby or Daisy but only of Jordan, sitting next to me.

"Daisy ought to have something nice in her life," said Jordan.

"Does she want to see Gatsby?"

"She's not supposed to know about it. He doesn't want her to know. You're just supposed to invite her to tea."

We passed a block of apartments, and they threw soft yellow light from the windows. I drew Jordan closer to me. She smiled her proud little smile, so I kissed her.

---

■be right next door すぐ隣である ■sort of 多少 ■go through with ～をやり通す、完遂する ■be supposed to ～することになっている、することが期待されている ■a block of apartment アパートの一棟

「不安なのよ。あまりにも長く待ったから。あなたが嫌がるんじゃないかと思ってるわ」

「きみに頼んだらいいじゃないか?」

「デイジーに家を見てもらいたいんですって。あなたの家はすぐ隣でしょ」

「なるほど!」

「ギャツビーとしては、デイジーがそのうちパーティーにふらりとやってくるのを期待してたと思う」ジョーダンは言った。「でも彼女は現れなかった。それで、色んな人にデイジーを知らないか聞きはじめた。彼が見つけた最初の1人が、私だったというわけ。図書室に呼び出されたあの夜のことよ。でもあなたがトムの友達だって教えたら、まったく気が進まなくなったみたいだった」

日が暮れていくなか、馬車でセントラル・パークを周るのは心地良かった。ふと気づけば、僕の頭にあるのはギャツビーでもデイジーでもなく、隣に座っているジョーダンのことだけだった。

「デイジーの人生にはもっと素敵なことがあっていいはずよ」ジョーダンは言った。

「デイジーはギャツビーに会いたがってるの?」

「彼女には知らせないことになってるの。ギャツビーが知られたくないっていうから。あなたはただデイジーをお茶に招待してあげて」

僕たちはアパートが並ぶ一画を通り過ぎた。どの部屋の窓も、黄色い柔らかな光を投げかけている。僕はジョーダンを引き寄せ、あのすました顔で微笑む彼女に口づけた。

# 9

That night when I came home, I saw Gatsby on his lawn. He saw me and walked over.

"Hello, old sport," he said. "Let's go to Coney Island. We'll go in my car."

"It's too late," I said.

"Well, how about going for a swim in my pool then?"

He sounded very eager to please me.

"I've got to go to bed," I said.

"All right." He stood there looking at me, as if he didn't want me to go in yet. I knew why he was hanging around—he wanted to know whether I was going to invite Daisy to tea.

"I talked with Miss Baker," I said. "I'm going to call Daisy tomorrow and invite her to come over to tea."

"Oh, that's all right," he said, trying to sound like he didn't care. "I don't want to trouble you."

"What day would be best for you?" I asked.

---

■Coney Island コニー・アイランド《遊園地と海水浴場があるレジャースポット》
■eager to しきりに〜したがる　■hang around うろつく　■whether 接 〜かどうか

# 9

 その夜、家に帰ってくると、隣の庭にギャツビーの姿が見えた。彼は僕に気づくと、歩いてやってきた。
「やあ、きみ」ギャツビーは言った。「これからコニー・アイランドに行きませんか。私の車で行きましょう」
「時間が遅すぎるよ」
「そうか、じゃあプールで泳ぐのはどうでしょう？」
 ギャツビーは僕の機嫌を取ろうと必死だった。
「もう寝ないといけないから」僕は言った。
「そうですね」ギャツビーはその場に立って、まだ行かないでほしいというように僕をじっと見た。彼がぐずぐずしている理由はわかっていた。僕がデイジーをお茶に招待する気があるかどうか、知りたいのだ。
「ベイカーさんと話したよ」僕は言った。「明日デイジーに電話をして、お茶に招待しようと思う」
「ああ、それは大丈夫です」ギャツビーは気にかけていない風を装って言った。「きみに迷惑をかけたくありませんし」
「きみはいつなら都合がいいんだい？」僕は聞いた。

"What day would be best for *you*?" he replied. "I really don't want to trouble you."

So we agreed on the day after tomorrow. But he insisted on paying somebody to cut my grass before she came. The next day, I called Daisy and invited her to tea. I told her not to bring Tom.

It was pouring rain on the day of the tea. In the morning, a man came to cut my grass in the heavy rain. Then Gatsby sent over many bunches of flowers, which his servants arranged all over my house. Then, about an hour later, Gatsby himself showed up at my door. He was wearing a white suit, a silver shirt, and a gold tie. He looked very pale and tired, as if he didn't get any sleep the night before.

He sat on a chair in my living room and looked very anxious for about half an hour. Then he suddenly got up and said he was going home.

"What?" I asked. "Why?"

"Nobody is coming to tea. It's too late!"

"Calm down," I said. "It's two minutes to four o'clock. She'll be here soon."

Just then, we heard a car coming up the road. We both jumped up. I went out into the yard. Daisy's car came slowly up to the house, and I saw her face smiling at me from the window.

■day after tomorrow 明後日　■insist on ～を強く主張する　■send over 送ってくる　■all over ～全体、くまなく　■show up 姿を見せる　■Calm down. 落ち着け。冷静になれ。

「きみこそいつなら都合がいいんですか?」ギャツビーは聞き返した。「本当に迷惑をかけたくないんですよ」

けっきょく、明後日にしようと2人で決めた。でもギャツビーは、デイジーが来る前に僕の家の芝刈りを手配させてくれと言ってきかなかった。翌日、僕はデイジーに電話をかけ、お茶に招待した。そして、トムを連れてこないように頼んだ。

約束の日は、雨が降りしきっていた。午前中、男が1人でやってきて、激しい雨の中で芝刈りをしていった。ギャツビーは大量の花を送ってきて、それを彼の使用人たちが僕の家のいたるところに飾った。それから1時間ほどして、ギャツビー本人が戸口に現われた。白いスーツに銀色のシャツ、金色のネクタイという出で立ちだった。昨夜はほとんど眠れなかったのか、顔は青白くやつれていた。

ギャツビーは僕の家の居間に腰を下ろし、ひどく不安そうにしていた。そうして30分あまりが過ぎると、いきなり立ち上がって帰ると言い出した。

「何だって? どうして?」僕は聞いた。

「誰もお茶には来ないよ。もう遅すぎる!」

「落ち着くんだ」僕は言った。「まだ4時2分前だ。彼女はもうすぐ来るさ」

ちょうどそのとき、車が近づいてくる音がして、僕たちは勢いよく立ちあがった。僕が庭へ出ていくと、デイジーの車がゆっくりこちらへ向かってくるところだった。車の窓の向こうから、デイジーが僕に微笑んでいるのがわかった。

"Is this where you live, my dearest one?" she asked me in her beautiful, musical voice.

"Yes, Daisy, do come in," I said. I took her hand and helped her out of the car. We went in. I was shocked to find the living room was empty. Gatsby was nowhere in sight.

"Well, that's funny!" I said.

"What's funny?" Daisy asked, looking around her. Then there was a light knock at the door. I went out and opened it. There stood Gatsby, as pale as death, standing with his hands stuck deep in his coat pockets. He was completely wet and he stared helplessly into my eyes. He must have gone out the back door and walked around the house.

Without saying anything, Gatsby walked past me and turned into the living room. My heart was beating hard as I listened to the silence that followed.

Then I heard a strange, almost painful laugh come from Daisy, and I heard her say, "Well, I'm certainly glad to see you again."

More silence followed. I couldn't stand it, so I joined them in the living room. Daisy sat stiff, straight, and scared on a chair. Gatsby leaned against the wall by a little shelf. He was trying to look natural and was doing a terrible job. As he leaned back, his head knocked over a clock on the little shelf, and he turned quickly and caught it.

"I'm sorry," he said to me.

■Do come in. どうぞお入りください。　■be nowhere in sight どこにも見えない　■turn into 進路を〜へ向ける　■silence that followed その後に続く静寂　■do a terrible job 功を奏さない、役に立たない　■knock over ひっくり返す

「私の大のお気に入りさん、ここがあなたのお家？」デイジーは、美しい音楽のような声で僕にたずねた。

　「そうだよ、デイジー。どうぞ中に入って」僕は車を降りる彼女に手を貸した。そして家の中に入り、愕然とした。居間に誰もいなかったのだ。ギャツビーは、どこにも見当たらなかった。

　「あれ、おかしいな！」

　「おかしいって何が？」デイジーが辺りを見回して言った。そこへ、軽いノックの音がした。僕が戸口へ行ってドアを開けると、死んだように青白い顔のギャツビーが、コートのポケットに深く両手を入れて立っていた。彼はすっかり濡れそぼって、心細げに僕の目を見つめた。裏口からこの家を出て、表まで回ってきたのだろう。

　ギャツビーは何も言わずに僕の横を通り過ぎ、居間へ入っていった。その後の沈黙に耳を澄ませながら、僕の心臓は激しく波打った。

　すると、何とも言えないデイジーの苦しげな笑い声が聞こえてきた。そしてこう言うのが聞こえた。「本当に嬉しいわ、あなたにまた会えたなんて」

　また沈黙が続いた。耐えきれずに、僕も居間に入った。デイジーはまっすぐ椅子に座ったまま固くなり、怯えていた。ギャツビーは、小さな棚の脇で壁に寄りかかっていた。何気ないふりをしていたが、あまりにも下手だった。ギャツビーが頭を動かした拍子に、棚の置き時計が倒れかけ、彼は慌てて振り返って手で押さえた。

　「すみません」ギャツビーは僕に言った。

Everybody was so uncomfortable that we didn't know what to do. Finally the maid came in from the kitchen carrying a tray with our tea. With the business of handing out cups and plates and pouring tea, we became a little more comfortable with each other. I took the first moment I could to excuse myself to leave Gatsby and Daisy alone.

"Where are you going?" asked Gatsby, looking very worried.

"I'll be back in a bit," I said. Then as I walked out the door, Gatsby followed me.

"Wait, I have to talk to you about something," he said. He and I hurried into the kitchen. Once the door closed behind us, Gatsby put his head in his hands.

"This was a mistake," he said, "a terrible, terrible mistake."

"Don't worry, you're just embarrassed," I said. "Daisy is embarrassed too."

"She is?" asked Gatsby. He didn't sound like he believed me.

"Yes, just as much as you are," I said. "You're acting like a little boy. Plus, you're being rude. Daisy is sitting in there all alone."

At that, Gatsby straightened up. He gave me a long look and walked back into the living room. I walked in the other direction, out the back door and into the yard. The rain was lighter now, and I was able to spend about half an hour comfortably under a big tree. After I felt that enough time had passed, I went back inside.

■business of 〜の業務　■take a moment 少し時間を取る　■in a bit すぐに　■all alone 1人きりで　■at that すると

3人とも落ち着かない気持ちで、どうしていいかわからずにいた。しばらくしてようやく、メイドがキッチンからお茶のトレイを運んできた。カップや皿が配られ、お茶が注がれるにつれ、お互いにいくらか緊張がほぐれてきた。ギャツビーとデイジーを2人きりにしようと、僕は頃合いを見て席を立った。

「どこへ行くんですか？」ギャツビーがひどく不安そうな顔で聞いた。
「すぐに戻ってくるよ」僕はそう答えて、部屋を出た。ギャツビーがついてきた。
「待ってください。話したいことがあるんです」僕たちは足早にキッチンへ入った。ドアを閉め切ると、ギャツビーは頭を両手で抱えた。

「これは間違いだ」ギャツビーは言った。「大きな、大きな間違いだ」
「心配するな。ちょっと気まずいだけだろう。デイジーだって気まずいはずだよ」
「彼女が？」ギャツビーは聞いた。僕の言うことが信じられない、という感じだった。
「そうさ。きみと同じくらいに」僕は言った。「まったく子どもみたいだな。それに失礼だぞ。デイジーを1人きりで待たせてるんだから」
　この一言に、ギャツビーははっとしたようだ。僕をしばらく見つめたあと、居間へ戻っていった。僕は逆の方へ進み、裏口から庭に出た。雨は弱くなっていたので、僕は大きな木の下で30分ほど濡れずに過ごすことができた。じゅうぶん時間をおいたと思った頃、家の中に戻った。

In the living room, I found a completely different scene from the one I had left. Daisy and Gatsby sat together, staring into each other's eyes. All their discomfort was gone. Daisy's face was covered with tears, and she began wiping them away as I walked in. Gatsby seemed to glow with happiness.

"Hello, old sport," he said. He smiled his big, beautiful smile at me.

"It stopped raining," I said.

"Has it?" He looked out the window and said to Daisy, "Well look at that! It stopped raining."

Daisy looked at him with big, happy eyes and smiled. "I'm so glad, Jay," she said.

"I want you and Daisy to come over to my house," said Gatsby. "I'd like to show her around."

Daisy went upstairs to wash her face, and Gatsby and I waited for her outside.

"My house looks nice, doesn't it?" Gatsby asked. "Look how it catches the light."

I agreed that it was very beautiful.

"It took me just three years to earn the money that bought it."

I realized I still didn't know what Gatsby did for work. When I asked, Gatsby said, "Oh, this and that. I was in the medicine business, then the oil business. But I'm not in either now."

■be covered with tears 涙で濡れる ■wipe 〜 away 〜をぬぐう ■glow with happiness 幸せに輝く ■show around 案内する ■catch light 日の光を受ける

居間に入ると、出てきたときとはまるで違う光景があった。デイジーとギャツビーが並んで座り、互いに見つめ合っている。さっきまでのぎこちなさは完全に消え去っていた。デイジーは涙で顔中を濡らし、僕が入っていくと、目もとを拭いはじめた。ギャツビーの顔は幸せに輝いていた。

「やあ、きみ」ギャツビーはそう言って、あの大きな美しい微笑みを僕にみせた。
「雨がやんだよ」僕は言った。
「本当に？」彼は窓の外を確かめると、デイジーに言った。「ほら見てごらん！　雨がやんだよ」
　デイジーは幸せそうな大きな目でギャツビーを見て微笑んだ。「本当に嬉しいわ、ジェイ」
「きみとデイジーに、うちに来てほしいんです」ギャツビーは言った。「彼女を案内したい」
　デイジーは化粧を直しに2階へ行った。ギャツビーと僕は家の外で彼女を待った。
「私の家はなかなかいいでしょう？」ギャツビーが僕に聞いた。「あの光の当たり具合を見てください」
　僕は本当に美しい家だ、と同意した。
「あの家を買う金を稼ぐのに、丸3年かかりました」
　僕はいまだにギャツビーの仕事を知らないことに気づいた。たずねると、ギャツビーはこう答えた。「まあ、いろいろです。医薬品関係とか、石油関係の仕事もしたけど、今はどちらもやっていません」

It was a strange and unclear answer. I still had the uneasy feeling that he made his money in some way that was against the law.

Then Daisy came out. "Your house is that huge place *there*?" she said in shock.

We walked to the house, taking our time through his big yard and crossing his beach. When we entered the house, it was strangely quiet. I expected party guests to pop up at every corner, but nobody was there. We walked through bedrooms, guest rooms, music rooms, and the library. It was all so grand that Daisy kept making little noises of surprise, saying how much she admired the house.

Gatsby never took his eyes off of Daisy. In fact, it seemed like he judged the worth of his many things by Daisy's responses to them. Sometimes, too, he looked around at his house in a surprised way, as though he couldn't believe all of it was his.

Gatsby's bedroom was the simplest room of all. Daisy walked about it in wonder. Gatsby opened his closet and showed us all his beautiful clothes inside. There were suits and ties and robes and piles of shirts folded neatly.

"I've got a man in England who buys my clothes. He sends a selection of things at the beginning of each season."

■against the law 法律違反で　■pop up 不意に現れる　■make a noise 声をあげる　■judge ~ by … ~を…で判断（評価）する　■walk about 歩き回る　■in wonder 驚嘆して

奇妙であいまいな答えだった。何か法に背くことをして稼いだのではないかという思いは、まだ拭えなかった。

　デイジーが家から出てきた。「あなたの家って、あのとっても大きな家?」彼女は驚いて言った。

　僕たちはギャツビー邸の広い庭と浜辺をゆっくり歩きながら邸宅に向かった。中に入ると、奇妙なほど静かだった。僕は部屋のあちこちからパーティー客が飛び出してくるような気がしていたが、そこには誰もいなかった。僕たちは寝室、来客用の寝室、音楽室、そして図書室を見て回った。そのあまりの大きさに、デイジーは驚きの声を小さくしきりに漏らし、なんて素敵なのと讃えていた。

　ギャツビーはデイジーから目を離さなかった。まるで、デイジーの反応を見て家のあらゆるものの価値を評価しているみたいだった。そしてときどき、ギャツビーは驚いたような目で家を見回した。それがすべて自分のものだとは信じられないかのように。

　ギャツビーの寝室は邸宅の中で一番質素な場所だった。デイジーはうっとりした様子で歩き回った。ギャツビーはクローゼットを開き、ずらりと並んだ美しい服を見せてくれた。スーツにネクタイ、ローブ、きちんとたたまれたシャツの山が詰め込まれている。

　「英国に、私のために服を見つくろってくれる男がいるんです。毎シーズンの初めに一式を送ってもらっています」

He laughed and took out a pile of shirts and began throwing them, one by one, before us. While we admired, he brought out more and more, and the soft, rich pile grew higher. Suddenly, Daisy bent her head into the shirts and began to cry.

"They're such beautiful shirts!" she said. "I've never seen such—such beautiful shirts before!" Her tears rolled down her face, and she smiled, so bright and so sad.

After that, we walked to the window and looked across the bay. It was raining lightly again.

"If it wasn't raining we could see your home across the bay," said Gatsby. "You always have a green light that burns all night at the end of your dock."

Daisy put her arm through his, but he didn't seem to notice. He was staring across the water. Perhaps he had just realized that the importance of that light had disappeared forever. Compared to the great distance that had separated them, that green light had always seemed very near to her—almost touching her. It had seemed as close as a star to the moon. Now that he had finally reached Daisy, it became just another light.

I looked around the room and saw a photograph that interested me. It was of an old man dressed in boat clothes.

"Who is this?" I asked.

"That's Mr. Dan Cody, old sport. He's dead now. He used to be my best friend years ago."

■bend one's head うなだれる ■look across 〜を眺める ■put one's arm through someone's （人と人とが）腕を組む ■stare across 〜越しに見つめる ■now that 今や〜だから ■It is of 〜だ《of ＋名詞の形容詞的用法》 ■used to be 以前は〜だった

ギャツビーは笑ってシャツの山を取り出すと、1枚ずつ僕たちの前に投げ出しはじめた。僕たちが見とれていると、ギャツビーはさらにシャツを出してきて、柔らかく贅沢な生地の山がどんどん高くなっていった。すると突然、デイジーがシャツの山に顔をうずめて泣き出した。

「なんて美しいシャツなの！　こんな——こんな美しいシャツを見たことないわ！」涙がデイジーの頬を流れ落ちた。デイジーは微笑み、とてもまばゆく、とても悲しそうだった。

　それから、僕たちは窓辺へ行き、入り江を眺めた。ふたたび弱い雨が降っていた。

「雨でなければ、入り江の向こうにきみの家が見える」ギャツビーは言った。「きみの家の桟橋の先には、いつも緑色の灯りが一晩中ついているでしょう」

　デイジーがギャツビーの腕に手を通したが、彼は気づいていないようだった。彼は海を見つめていた。おそらく、緑色の灯りの持つ大きな意味が永遠に失われたことにいま気づいたのだろう。2人を隔てる果てしない距離に比べたら、緑の灯りはいつも彼女のすぐそばに——触れそうなほど近くに——あるように見えた。月にとっての星ほどに近く感じられたのだ。だが、デイジーに手が届いた今ではただの灯りでしかない。

　部屋を見回すと、気になる写真が目に入った。ヨット用の服を着た年配の男性の写真だ。

「この人は？」僕は聞いた。

「ダン・コーディーさんだよ、きみ。もう亡くなった。何年も前、私の一番の友人だったんです」

"Come here, quick!" said Daisy, who was still at the window. We went over and looked. The rain had just stopped and the sun was setting, streaming bright light through pink and gold clouds.

"Look at that, Jay," Daisy whispered. "I'd like to get one of those pink clouds and put you in it and push you around."

As Daisy and Gatsby stood there, I decided to go home. I started to say goodbye but stopped myself. I noticed something in Gatsby's face. He looked ever so slightly troubled, as if he were puzzled about something. I realized then that Daisy, no matter how lovely she was, could never be as perfect as Gatsby had made her in his mind. It was not her fault. Too much time had passed — Gatsby had waited five long years! In every memory of her, he had made her greater and lovelier than any human ever could be. Now, perhaps he was beginning to realize the difference between his imagined Daisy and his real one. I watched him as he took her hand. Then Daisy said something into his ear and he looked at her with a rush of emotion. Her voice, beautiful and musical, was one thing that could not be over-dreamed. Her voice was better than any imagined song.

They continued to look out the window. They had forgotten me. I looked once more at them and quietly walked home, leaving them there together.

■push ~ around ~を振り回す ■ever so slightly ごくわずかに ■puzzle about ~に頭を悩ませる ■no matter how どんなに~であろうとも ■say into one's ear 耳元で言う ■with a rush of emotion あふれるような興奮とともに

「ねえ来て、早く!」まだ窓辺にいるデイジーが声を上げた。行ってみると、雨がちょうど上がり、ピンク色と黄金色に輝く雲の隙間から夕陽が光を放っていた。

「あれを見て、ジェイ」デイジーがささやく。「あのピンクの雲を1つとって、その中にあなたをしまって、あちこちつっつきたいわ」

デイジーとギャツビーがそこに立っているうちに、僕は帰ることにした。でもさよならを言おうとした瞬間、口をつぐんだ。ギャツビーの表情に変化が見てとれたからだ。何かに困惑しているような表情が、かすかに浮かんでいた。そのとき僕は気がついた。デイジーがいかに美しくても、ギャツビーが心に描いてきたデイジーのように完璧にはなれないことに。それはデイジーのせいではない。あまりに長い時間がたってしまったせいだ——ギャツビーは5年も待ったのだから! あらゆるデイジーの記憶をもとに、ギャツビーはどんな人間よりも素晴しく愛らしいデイジー像をつくっていった。きっと彼はこのとき、思い描いていたデイジーと実像との違いを実感しはじめていたのだろう。僕はギャツビーがデイジーの手を取るのを見ていた。デイジーが耳元に何かささやくと、彼は感情が込み上げたように彼女を見返した。デイジーの音楽のような声の美しさだけは、どんな夢も越えられはしない。彼女の声は、どんな幻想の歌よりも美しかった。

2人は窓の外をずっと眺めていた。僕がいることは忘れたようだ。僕はもう一度2人を見てから、静かに歩いて家に戻った。窓辺に並ぶ2人を残したまま。

# 覚えておきたい英語表現

> I'm afraid I made you rather angry in the car earlier. (p.96, 8行目)
> 今朝ドライブ中にあなたを少々怒らせてしまったのではと思っています。

**【解説】**be afraid (that) ～「～ではないかと心配している」の熟語です。afraidは「恐れている」という意味の形容詞ですが、"I'm afraid (that)～"と使う場合は、「ちょっと言いにくいのだけど～」「残念ながら～」「申し訳ないけど～」という、話し手の気持ちを伝える表現になります。

この言葉からは、"ニックの機嫌を損ねてしまったのでは"という「自覚があり、申し訳ないと思っている」というギャツビーの心情を読みとることができます。

> I'm afraid that I can't go to the party.
> 申し訳ないのですがパーティーには出席できません。

> I'm afraid (that) it will rain tomorrow.
> (残念ながら)明日は雨だろうね。

> "Is she sick in bed?" "I'm afraid so."
> 「彼女寝込んでるの?」「そうらしいよ」

> "Can I win the next game?" "I'm afraid not."
> 「次の試合勝てるかな?」「ちょっと無理かもね」

> ... he must have been the young officer in her white car. (p.106, 9行目)
> 彼がデイジーの白い車に乗っていた若い将校に違いない。

**【解説】**must have 過去分詞で「～したに違いない」の意味になります。「助動詞＋現在完了形」のセットで慣用的な意味を表します。ぜひ覚えましょう。

| | |
|---|---|
| Tom must have missed the bus. | トムはバスに乗り遅れたに違いない。 |
| Tom may have missed the bus. | トムはバスに乗り遅れたかもしれない。 |
| Tom can't have missed the bus. | トムはバスに乗り遅れたはずがない。 |

---

It took me just three years to earn the money that bought it.
(p.118, 下から4行目)
これを手に入れる資金を稼ぐのにちょうど3年かかりましたよ。

---

【解説】It takes＋人＋時間＋to Vで、「〜がVするのに……かかる」の意味になります。Itは形式主語といい、形だけの主語でto V（to不定詞）以下のことを指しています。だからto V以下を主語に持ってくると、

To earn money that bought it took me just three years.
(直訳)これを買う資金を稼ぐことは私にちょうど3年を費やさせた。

となるわけですが、この英文だと何だか読みづらいですよね？　主語（主部）が大きくなると読みづらくなるのです。形式主語「It」が用いられることで、文が頭でっかち（主語が大きい）にならずに読みやすくなります。「時間がかかる」の動詞はtake、「お金がかかる」はcostを使います。

It took me a year to get the driving license.
自動車免許を取るのに1年かかったよ。

It took me only five minutes to drive here.
ここまで車でたったの5分だったよ。

It cost us a million dollars to build the school.
学校建設に1億円かかった。

　デイジーに釣り合う男になるために、壮麗な豪邸を手に入れたギャツビー。恋に燃えるギャツビーにとっては3年「も」かかったのでしょうが、同じく一旗あげようと思ってNYにやってきたニックにとっては、どうやったら「わずか」3年でこれだけ

の大金を稼げるのかという疑問が浮かんだかもしれません。

"I was in the medicine business, then the oil business. ~ "というギャツビーの言葉をニックはほとんど信じていませんよね？

ギャツビーの派手な暮らし、絢爛豪華なパーティー、そしてそれを支える出所不明の資金……、全ては貧しさゆえに失ったデイジーの愛を取り戻すためでした。純粋すぎるくらい一途なギャツビーの情熱と行動が、どこか切なくて虚しさを感じさせるところに、「ロストジェネレーション（失われた世代）」らしい空気感が漂っているように思えてなりません。

# Part 4

# 10

Gatsby told me much later that his name was actually James Gatz. He was from North Dakota, and his parents were poor farming people. They led a life that he didn't want, and in his own mind, he never quite accepted that they were his parents at all.

When James Gatz was sixteen years old, he left home to find a new life for himself. He already had a new name picked out—Jay Gatsby. The first person he told it to was Dan Cody.

For about a year, Gatsby had been working around Lake Superior, fishing and helping people with their boats. But every day, he imagined a beautiful future for himself. He imagined huge houses, wealth, and riches. Every day, he added another beautiful detail to his dream.

One day, as he was walking along the beach looking for something to do, he came across Dan Cody's large yacht. Cody was stopped there for the night, but Gatsby knew a dangerous storm was coming. Cody was fifty years old then, and very, very rich.

■lead a life 人生を送る ■in one's own mind 心の中では ■pick out 選ぶ ■Lake Superior スペリオル湖《北アメリカの五大湖の１つ》 ■come across ～に偶然出くわす

# 10

　ギャツビーはずいぶん後になって、本当の名前はジェイムズ・ギャッツだと教えてくれた。ノースダコタ州の生まれで、両親は貧しい農夫だった。彼は親の生き方に納得できず、心の中では、2人を両親だと思うことはいっさいなかったという。

　16歳になったジェイムズ・ギャッツは、家を出て、新しい人生を始める道を選んだ。新しい名前はもう決めていた――ジェイ・ギャツビー。その名を初めて告げた相手がダン・コーディーだった。

　1年ほど、ギャツビーはスペリオル湖の周辺で働き、漁をしたり、船の世話をしたりして暮らしていた。だが、自分の輝かしい未来を夢見ない日はなかった。大きな邸宅や、財産、豊かさに憧れた。日を追うごとに、その夢の細部が継ぎ足され膨らんでいった。

　ある日、何かすることはないかと浜辺を歩いていたギャツビーは、ダン・コーディーの大きなヨットに気がついた。コーディーはその夜、ヨットを湖岸に停めておくつもりだったが、ギャツビーは激しい嵐が来ることを知っていた。コーディーはこのとき50歳。そしてとてつもない金持ちだった。

Gatsby saw an opportunity. He borrowed a rowboat and rowed over to Cody's yacht. He introduced himself as Jay Gatsby and told Cody he better move to a safer place because of the storm that was quickly approaching.

Cody was traveling alone. His wife had married him for his money and was not a very nice woman. So for five years, he had been moving from place to place in his yacht trying to seek some happiness. And suddenly, here was this young man who was smart, independent, and eager to help. Cody liked Gatsby instantly. After asking Gatsby a few questions, Cody decided to hire him. A few days later, Cody took Gatsby into town and bought him a blue coat, six pairs of white pants, and a hat. When the yacht left for the West Indies, Gatsby went too.

Gatsby was hired to do many things for Cody, including some rather personal work. Cody liked to drink, and he knew he made bad decisions when he drank too much. So, one of Gatsby's jobs was to make sure Cody stayed in his room when he drank. The two men enjoyed having each other around, and Gatsby worked for Cody for five years. During that time, they traveled all over the world. But it all ended when Cody's wife came onto the yacht in Boston one day, and Cody died a week later.

Cody had left Gatsby twenty-five thousand dollars, but Gatsby never got it. Cody's wife somehow managed to get all of Cody's money, which totaled several million dollars.

■see an opportunity 好機であると思う ■better do 〜したほうがよい ■from place to place あちこちに ■make sure 確実に〜にする ■have each other around （仲間同士が）お互いそばにいる ■manage to 何とか〜する

ギャツビーはチャンスを見出した。彼は手漕ぎのボートを借りて、コーディーのヨットまで漕いでいった。そして自分はジェイ・ギャツビーだと名乗り、嵐が近づいているから安全な場所に移した方がいいと教えた。

コーディーは1人で旅をしていた。結婚した妻はコーディーの金が目当てで、あまりいい女ではなかった。それで5年ほど、幸せを求めてあちこちをヨットで回っているところだった。そんなとき、ふいに若い青年が目の前に現われたのだ。頭がよく、自立していて、役に立ちたいという意欲を感じさせる若者。コーディーはすぐにギャツビーを気に入った。いくつか質問をしたのち、ギャツビーを雇うことに決めた。数日後、コーディーはギャツビーを町に連れていき、青い上着と白いズボンを6本、それに帽子を買ってやった。ヨットが西インド諸島へ出発するときには、ギャツビーもその船上にいた。

コーディーはギャツビーに色々な仕事をやらせた。なかには個人的なものもあった。コーディーは酒好きで、酔うとろくでもない真似をすると自分でわかっていた。だから酒を飲むときは、自分が大人しく部屋にいるようにギャツビーに見張らせた。2人はいい関係を築きあい、ギャツビーはコーディーのもとで5年間働いた。そしてその間に世界中を旅した。しかし、その日々はいつまでも続かなかった。コーディーの妻がボストンでヨットに乗り込んできて、その1週間後にコーディーが死んだのだ。

コーディーはギャツビーに2万5000ドルの現金を遺したが、ギャツビーの手元に渡ることはなかった。コーディーの妻が数百万ドルにのぼる全財産を手に入れようと画策したためだった。

# 11

One day later that summer, Gatsby finally met Tom. It happened by accident—Tom was riding horses with two of his friends, and they rode onto Gatsby's land without knowing it. I was there, visiting Gatsby. He invited them inside and we all sat down for a drink.

"I'm delighted to see you," said Gatsby, shaking Tom's hand. "We're neighbors. Please, sit down. What can I get you to drink?"

Gatsby watched Tom closely. Tom, of course, had no idea who Gatsby was. At some point while we all talked, Gatsby said to Tom, "I know your wife." I paused and stared. It seemed like Gatsby was testing Tom somehow.

"Oh, do you?" asked Tom. Then he turned to me. "You live near here, Nick?"

"Next door," I said.

■by accident 偶然に　■without knowing it そうとは知らずに　■be delighted to 〜して光栄である　■get 〜 to … 〜に…してもらう

# 11

　あの夏のある日、とうとうギャツビーとトムが顔を合わせることになった。そうなったのは偶然で、トムが友人2人と乗馬をしていたら、知らずにギャツビー邸の敷地に入ってしまったのだ。そのとき、僕はギャツビーの家を訪ねていた。ギャツビーは1杯いかがですか、とトムたちを招き入れた。

　「お会いできて光栄です」ギャツビーはトムと握手をして言った。「近くに住んでいますからね。どうぞお掛けください。何を飲まれますか？」

　ギャツビーはトムをじっと見つめた。トムはもちろん、ギャツビーが誰なのかまるでわかっていなかった。みんなで話しているときに、ギャツビーが「あなたの奥さまを知っています」とトムに言った。僕は息をのんでギャツビーを見つめた。まるでトムを試しているみたいだった。

　「そうなんですか？」トムはそう言って、僕の方を向いた。「きみの家はこの近くだろう、ニック？」

　「隣だよ」僕は答えた。

Tom and his friends left shortly afterward. But that Saturday, Tom and Daisy finally came to one of Gatsby's parties. They arrived just as it was getting dark, and Gatsby and I met them out in the yard. We walked among crowds of people toward the house.

"This is so exciting!" Daisy said.

"Look around," said Gatsby, "you must recognize some of the people here. There are many famous people here tonight. Singers, actors, politicians..."

"Well, we don't know many famous people," Tom said.

"What about her?" asked Gatsby, pointing to a very beautiful woman sitting under a tree. Tom and Daisy stared in shock. She was a famous movie star, perhaps one of the most famous at the time.

We wandered around, eating and drinking. Tom began talking with a group of people, and Daisy and Gatsby danced. I watched them and was surprised at what a good dancer Gatsby was. Then the two walked over to my house and sat on the steps for half an hour. I stayed in the garden and watched for anybody who might come that way.

As we were sitting down to dinner, Tom appeared again.

"Do you mind if I eat with those people over there?" he asked. "There's a man who's saying some interesting things..."

---

■out in the yard 庭で　■look around 辺りを見回す　■wander around ブラブラ歩き回る　■walk over to ～の方まで歩いて行く　■Do you mind if ～? ～しても構いませんか？

トムと友人たちはそれから間もなく帰った。だがその土曜日、トムとデイジーがついにギャツビーのパーティーに現われた。暗くなりかけた頃にやってきた2人を、ギャツビーと僕は庭で出迎えた。客がひしめき合う中を4人で邸宅に向かって歩いた。

「とってもわくわくするわ！」デイジーが言った。
「見回してみてください」ギャツビーが言った。「きっと見たことのある人がいますよ。今夜は有名人が何人も来ていますから。歌手、俳優、政治家とか……」
「いや、僕たちはあまり有名人を知らないのでね」トムが言った。
「あの女性はどうです？」ギャツビーが木の下に座っているひときわ美しい女性を指した。トムとデイジーは目を見張った。女性は当時だれもが知る映画女優だった。

　僕たちは歩き回りながら、食べたり飲んだりした。トムが他の客たちと話をはじめたので、デイジーとギャツビーはダンスをした。2人を眺めていて、僕はギャツビーの踊りのうまさに驚いた。それから2人は僕の家の方へ歩いていき、玄関前の階段に腰を下ろして30分ほど過ごした。僕はギャツビーの庭に残って、誰かがそっちへ行かないよう見張っていた。

　その後、3人で食事をしていると、トムが戻ってきた。
「向こうの人たちと食事をしてきてもいいかな？」トムは聞いた。「ちょっと面白い話をしてくれる男がいてね……」

"Go ahead," said Daisy. Then she watched as Tom went to sit with a girl, not a man as he had said.

"She's rather pretty," Daisy said. I knew then that aside from the time she had spent with Gatsby, she was not having a good time. We were sitting at a table with very drunk people. That was my fault, because I knew them and had had a good time with them here a few weeks before. But what seemed fun a few weeks ago now seemed to be in bad taste. A girl was very drunk and was trying to lean her head on my shoulder. An older woman was talking very loudly about how the girl always drank too much. Daisy, who didn't drink at all, seemed very uncomfortable.

The evening went on in this way. When Daisy and Tom decided to leave, I waited with them for their car.

"What does this Gatsby do for work, anyway?" asked Tom. "What is he, some big gangster?"

"No, he owned a bunch of stores that sold medicine," said Daisy. "The stores made him very rich."

"Most of these newly rich people are just big gangsters," Tom said. "And he must have worked hard to get this crazy scene together. Daisy didn't like it," he said to me. "Did you see her face when that drunk girl almost fell over her?"

---

■Go ahead. どうぞ。　■then that そのとき　■aside from ～を除いては　■in bad taste 品のない、悪趣味な　■fall over ～に倒れかかる

「ええ、どうぞ」デイジーは答えた。トムの姿を目で追い、じっさいには男ではなく若い女の隣に座るのを見届けた。

「そこそこ美人ね」デイジーは言った。ギャツビーと過ごした時間を除いては、デイジーがパーティーを楽しんでいないことに僕は気づいた。僕らと同じテーブルについた客たちはひどい酔っ払いだった。これは僕が悪い。数週間前のパーティーで知り合ったときは楽しかったので一緒に座ったのだが、それが今では下品にしか思えなかった。若い女は酔っ払って僕の肩に頭を乗せようとし、年配の女は、いつもその娘が飲みすぎると大声でまくし立てた。まったく酒を飲まないデイジーは、いかにも居心地が悪そうだった。

こうして夜が過ぎていった。デイジーとトムが帰ることになり、車が用意されるまで僕も一緒に待った。

「ギャツビーってやつは、いったい何の仕事をしてるんだ？ 大物ギャングか何かか？」トムは聞いた。

「違うわ。ドラッグストアをいくつも経営していて、それで大きな財産を築いたの」デイジーが言った。

「この手の成金は、たいていがギャングさ。これだけの顔を揃えるのにさぞ頑張ったんだろうな。デイジーは気に入ってなかったよ」トムは僕に言った。「酔った娘に倒れ込まれそうになったときのデイジーの顔を見たかい？」

Daisy didn't respond and started to sing. Her strange, beautiful voice carried on the wind until their car arrived and they left.

I stayed at Gatsby's house. He had asked me to wait for him until he was free. Finally, when the last guest had gone upstairs and the last bedroom light turned off, Gatsby came to find me.

"She didn't like it," he said immediately.

"Of course she did."

"No, she didn't. She didn't have a good time," he insisted. "I feel far away from her. It's hard to make her understand."

I knew what Gatsby wanted. He wanted Daisy to tell Tom, "I never loved you." After she destroyed their four years of marriage like this, Gatsby wanted to take her back to Louisville where they would get married. It would be like their five years apart never happened.

"She doesn't understand," he said. "She used to be able to understand. We would sit for hours—"

He broke off and started walking down a dark path covered in crushed flowers and broken glass.

"Don't ask too much of her," I said. "You can't repeat the past."

"Can't repeat the past?" he cried in shock. "Why of course you can!" He looked around wildly, as if he was looking for the past hiding right there in his garden.

■carry 動（声などが）伝わる　■turn off（灯りを）消す　■make someone understand（人に）自分の考えを伝える　■take ~ back ~を取り戻す　■break off 中断する　■ask too much of ~に無理難題を言う

デイジーは何も言わず、歌を口ずさみだした。彼女の不思議な美しい声が風に乗った。やがて車がきて、2人は帰っていった。
　僕はギャツビー邸に残った。手が空くまで待っていてほしいと言われていたのだ。ようやく最後の客が2階へ行き、来客用の寝室の灯りがすべて消えると、ギャツビーが僕のところへやってきた。
　「彼女、気に入らなかったみたいだ」ギャツビーはいきなり言った。
　「まさか、気に入ってたさ」
　「いや、ちがう。楽しんでいなかったよ」ギャツビーは言い張った。「彼女をものすごく遠く感じた。わかってもらうのは簡単じゃない」
　ギャツビーが何を望んでいるかはわかった。彼の望みは、デイジーがトムに「あなたを愛したことはなかった」と告げることだ。そうして4年間の結婚生活を壊させた後で、ギャツビーはデイジーを取り戻し、ルイヴィルで結婚しようとしている。そうなれば、互いに離れていた5年間などなかったように思えるだろう。
　「彼女はわかってくれない」ギャツビーは言った。「昔の彼女ならわかってくれたのに。2人で座って何時間も……」
　彼は言いかけたまま口を閉ざし、踏みつぶされた花やガラスの破片が散らばる暗い小道を歩きだした。
　「彼女に求めすぎたらだめだよ」僕は言った。「過去は繰り返せない」
　「過去は繰り返せない？」ギャツビーは驚いたように声を上げた。「繰り返せないわけがない！」ギャツビーはあたりを慌ただしく見回した。この庭のどこかに隠れている過去を見つけ出そうとするように。

# 12

All of a sudden, there were no more parties at Gatsby's house. Every weekend throughout the summer, there had been bright lights and laughter and music at his house. Now there was nothing but silence.

I went over there one afternoon to see if he was all right. A mean-looking man answered his door.

"Is Mr. Gatsby sick?" I asked.

"No," said the man.

"I haven't seen him lately, and I was a little worried. Please tell him Mr. Carraway came over," I said.

The man agreed and shut the door in my face. I found out later that Gatsby had let every servant in his house go. He had replaced them with about six new people that no one had ever seen before. They did not go into to town to order food or drink. People in town said that the people were not servants at all.

The next day, Gatsby called me on the phone.

■all of a sudden 突然 ■nothing but ただ〜だけ ■mean-looking 形 意地悪そうな ■in one's face 目の前で ■let 〜 go 〜を解雇する ■replace 〜 with … 〜を…と入れ替える

# 12

　ギャツビー邸でのパーティーはぱたりとなくなった。夏のあいだ、週末は必ずまばゆい灯りと笑い声と音楽があったのに、今はただ沈黙があるだけだった。

　ある日の午後、僕はギャツビーの様子を見にいった。強面(こわもて)の男がドアを開けた。
「ギャツビーさんは具合が悪いのでしょうか？」僕は聞いた。
「いいや」男は答えた。
「この頃見かけないものですから、少し心配で。キャラウェイが来たとお伝えください」
　男は頷いて、ドアをばたんと閉めた。後になって、ギャツビーが使用人たちをすべて辞めさせたと知った。かわりに、誰も顔を見たことのない6人を家に置いた。彼らは町へ行って食糧や飲み物を買いつけることはなく、使用人とは程遠い連中だと噂されていた。

　明くる日、ギャツビーから電話があった。

"Are you going away?" I asked. "I heard you fired all your servants."

"I wanted people who wouldn't talk about my private matters to others," he said, "because Daisy comes over quite often in the afternoons now. So I hired some people that Wolfsheim knows."

"I see," I said.

Then he told me that Daisy wanted me to come to her house for lunch the next day. Miss Baker would be there too, he said.

The next day was hot—it was one of the last days of summer, and it was definitely the hottest day of the year. Gatsby and I went together to Daisy's house. When we entered the living room, Daisy and Jordan were both dressed in white and laying on the couch.

"It's too hot to move!" they both said.

Tom entered the room. He saw us and greeted Gatsby first. He hid his dislike for him well.

"Mr. Gatsby!" he said, holding out his hand. "I'm glad to see you, sir."

"Make us a cold drink!" cried Daisy.

As Tom left the room again, Daisy got up and went over to Gatsby. She pulled his face down and kissed him on the mouth.

"You know I love you," she said to him.

---

■go away どこかへ行く、退去する ■too ~ to do ~すぎて…できない ■hold out （腕を）伸ばす ■You know ~. ご存知の通り~です

「ここを出ていくつもりなのか？」僕は聞いた。「使用人をみんな辞めさせたと聞いたけど」
「私の個人的なことをしゃべらない人間をそばに置こうと思ったんです」とギャツビーは言った。「最近はデイジーが午後によく来るからね。それでウルフシャイムのつてで人を雇いまた」
「なるほど」
ギャツビーは、明日、デイジーが僕を昼食に招待したいそうだと言った。ベイカーさんも一緒だという。
次の日は暑かった――夏の終わりで、あの年の一番暑い日だったと思う。僕はギャツビーと一緒にデイジーの家に行った。居間に入ると、デイジーとジョーダンが2人とも白い服を着て、カウチに横たわっていた。


「暑すぎて動けない！」2人が言った。
トムが部屋に入ってきた。僕たちを見ると、先にギャツビーに挨拶をした。彼への嫌悪をうまく隠していた。
「ギャツビーさん！」トムは手を差し出した。「またお会いできて嬉しいですよ」
「冷たい飲み物をお願い！」デイジーが声を上げた。
トムがふたたび部屋を出ていくと、デイジーが立ちあがってギャツビーに歩み寄った。そして、顔を引き寄せて口づけた。
「わかるでしょ、愛してること」

"You forget there are other people in the room," said Jordan, lightly laughing.

"I don't care!" said Daisy, smiling. But she sat back down next to Jordan on the couch. Just then Tom entered again with four full glasses. We all took one and drank them quickly, the ice knocking against the glass. We had lunch outside in the shade. There was an anxious kind of feeling all throughout lunch, and it made me uncomfortable.

"What will we do with ourselves this afternoon?" asked Daisy when we had finished. Jordan and I looked at her. Tom was having a conversation with Gatsby.

"I know! Let's go into town!" cried Daisy.

Tom just kept talking to Gatsby, not paying any attention to her.

"Who wants to go into town?" Daisy demanded. Gatsby's eyes floated toward her. "Ah," she cried, "you look so cool."

Their eyes met, and they stared at each other, as if they were alone. Daisy finally forced herself to look down at the table.

"You always look so cool," she repeated.

In that little moment, Daisy had silently told Gatsby that she loved him, and Tom Buchanan saw it. He was shocked. His mouth opened a little, and he just looked at Gatsby, and then back at Daisy.

■What will we do with ourselves? 私たちこれからどうしましょうか？　■I know! いい考えがあります！　■pay attention to ～に注意を払う　■force oneself to どうにかして～する

「この部屋はあなたたち2人きりじゃないのよ」ジョーダンは軽く笑って言った。
「気にしないもの！」デイジーは微笑んで言ったが、またジョーダンの隣に腰を下ろした。ちょうどそこへ、トムが酒をなみなみ注いだグラスを4つ持って戻ってきた。僕たちは1人ずつグラスをとり、一気に飲み干した。グラスに氷があたる音が鳴った。昼食は外の日陰でとった。食事のあいだずっと不穏な雰囲気があり、僕は落ち着かなかった。

「私たち、午後は何をしようかしら？」昼食を終えると、デイジーがたずねた。ジョーダンと僕は彼女を見た。トムはギャツビーと話をしていた。

「そうだわ！ 街へ行きましょう！」デイジーが言った。
トムはギャツビーと話をつづけ、デイジーの言うことに耳を傾けなかった。
「さあ、街へ行きたい人は？」デイジーが返事を促した。ギャツビーの視線がデイジーの方へさまよった。「ああ」と彼女は言った。「あなたっていつも涼しげね」
2人の目が合い、まるで2人きりでいるように、しばし見つめ合った。デイジーはやっとのことで視線をテーブルに落とした。
「あなたはいつも涼しげだわ」彼女は繰り返した。
そのちょっとした瞬間に、デイジーは無言でギャツビーに愛を告げていた。トム・ブキャナンはそれを見てとり、唖然とした。口をわずかに開いたままギャツビーを見て、それからまたデイジーを見た。

"All right," Tom said. "Let's go to town. Come on, we're all going to town."

He stood up suddenly, his eyes still flashing between Daisy and Gatsby. No one moved.

"Come on!" he said angrily. "What's the matter? If we're going to town, let's go now!"

Tom's hand, shaking a little, brought his glass to his lips and he took another drink. We all moved out to where the cars were parked.

"Shall we all go in my car?" Gatsby asked.

"No," said Tom. "You take my car and I'll take yours. Come on, Daisy. I'll drive you in this crazy yellow thing."

"No, you take Jordan and Nick," Daisy said. "I'll go with Gatsby." She walked close to Gatsby. As they got into Tom's little blue car, Jordan, Tom, and I got into Gatsby's. Tom started the car and sped off, leaving Daisy and Gatsby in the dust.

"Did you see that?" he demanded, as we got on the road.

"See what?"

He looked at Jordan and me with narrowed eyes. He realized that we must have known about Daisy and Gatsby all along.

■move out 家を出る　■Shall we ～?　～しましょうよ。　■take one's car 車に乗る
■this crazy yellow thing この馬鹿げた黄色いやつ（車）　■speed off （車を）飛ばす
■all along 最初からずっと

「わかった」トムは言った。「街へ行こう。みんなで街へ行こうじゃないか」

トムはだしぬけに立ち上がり、デイジーとギャツビーを素早く交互に見た。誰も動こうとしなった。

「さあ、ほら！」トムは怒ったように言った。「いったいどうしたんだ？ 街へ行くなら、さっさと行こう！」

トムは、かすかに震える手でグラスを口元に運び、酒を飲んだ。僕たちは外へ出て、車を止めてある場所へ向かった。

「みんなで僕の車で行きますか？」ギャツビーが聞いた。

「いや、」トムが言った。「あなたは私の車で、私はあなたの車で行こう。さあ、デイジー。このばかげた黄色いやつにきみを乗せよう」

「いやよ、あなたはジョーダンとニックを乗せていって」デイジーは言った。「私はギャツビーと行く」彼女はギャツビーのそばに行った。2人がトムの小さな青い車に乗り込むと、ジョーダン、トム、そして僕はギャツビーの車に乗り込んだ。トムが勢いよく車を発進させ、デイジーとギャツビーを砂ぼこりの中に残していった。

「あれを見たかい？」道路に出ると、トムが言った。

「あれって？」

トムは、ジョーダンと僕をいぶかしむように細い目で見た。デイジーとギャツビーのことを僕たちがずっと知っていたに違いないと気づいたのだ。

"You must think I'm blind, don't you?" he said. "Well I know some things when I see it, and I never liked that man! And I've found out some things about him. I would have found out more if I had known..."

"Tom, if you didn't like him why did you invite him to lunch?" Jordan demanded.

"I didn't! Daisy did! She knew him before we were married—I hate to think how they ever met."

We drove along unhappily in the heat. When the eyes of Doctor T. J. Eckleburg came into sight, I reminded Tom that we needed gas. He pulled off the road angrily and stopped at Wilson's garage. After a while, Wilson appeared at the door and stared at the car.

"We want some gas!" Tom cried out. "What do you think we stopped for? To admire the view?"

"I'm sick," said Wilson. He didn't move. His face looked green and he truly looked ill.

"Well, do I need to help myself?" Tom shouted. With an effort, Wilson walked over to the car and helped us with the gas.

"How do you like this car?" Tom asked Wilson.

"It's a nice yellow one," Wilson said, working with the gas.

"I'll sell you this one instead of my blue car," said Tom. "How about it?"

---

■hate to 〜したくない(がせざるを得ない)　■gas 图ガソリン　■look green 青ざめている　■help oneself 自分でやる　■How do you like 〜？ 〜をどう思いますか？

「僕には何も見えてないと思ってるんだろう？」トムは言った。「だがな、僕も見れば分かることがある。それにあの男は初めから好かないんだ。あの男についてはいくらか調べてある。もっと調べることもできたんだ、もし……」

「トム、彼が気に入らないならどうして昼食に誘ったの？」ジョーダンが聞いた。

「僕は誘ってない！ 誘ったのはデイジーさ。僕と結婚する前からあいつを知っているそうだ。どんな出会いかなんて考えたくもない」

暑さの中、僕たちは不機嫌な気持ちで走り続けた。T・J・エックルバーグ博士の目が見えてくると、僕はトムに給油した方がいいと声をかけた。トムはいらいらした様子でハンドルを切り、ウィルソンの修理工場の前に車を止めた。しばらくして、ウィルソンが戸口に現われ、車をじっと見つめた。

「ガソリンを入れてくれよ！」トムが叫んだ。「他に何しに来たと思う？ 景色を楽しみにか？」

「私は病気なんです」ウィルソンは言った。彼はじっと動かなかった。顔色は青く、本当に具合が悪そうだった。

「なんだ、自分でやれって言うのか？」トムは怒鳴った。ウィルソンは車のところまでどうにか歩いてくると、ガソリンを入れてくれた。

「この車をどう思う？」トムはウィルソンに聞いた。

「素敵な黄色の車ですね」ウィルソンは給油をしながら答えた。

「僕の青い車の代わりに、こいつを売ろう」トムは言った。「それでどうだ？」

"I can't afford this," said Wilson, "but I would like to buy your other car. I need it soon. I'm taking my wife away from here."

Now Tom looked shocked.

"Taking her away? Where? And why?"

Wilson finished with the gas. "She's been telling me for the past ten years that she wants to go out West. Now I'm taking her there whether she wants to go or not."

"Why?" asked Tom again.

"Because I just found out that she's been fooling around with some other man around here."

Tom stared for a moment. Then he asked, "How much do I owe you for the gas?"

"A dollar and twenty cents."

Just then, I got the feeling that we were being watched. I looked up at Wilson's garage and noticed that Myrtle was watching us from a window. I watched as the look on her face changed from shock to anger to something else—was it jealousy? Then I realized her eyes were not fixed on Tom, but on Jordan Baker, whom she assumed was his wife.

---

■take ～ away ～を連れ去る　■finish with（仕事など）～を終える　■fool around with ～と不倫する　■How much do I owe you? おいくらですか？　■eyes are fixed on 目が～に釘付けである

「とても手が出ません」ウィルソンは言った。「でも、あなたのもう1台の車なら買います。すぐにでも必要なんです。妻をここから連れ出すので」

トムが驚きの表情をみせた。

「連れ出す？ どこへ？ なぜなんだ？」

ウィルソンは給油を終えた。「妻は10年前から西部に行きたいと言っていましてね。私は妻が望もうと望むまいと、向こうへ連れていくつもりです」

「なぜだ？」トムはまた聞いた。

「妻が浮気していたことを最近知ったからです。この辺りの男とね」

トムはしばらくウィルソンを見つめ、そして聞いた。「ガソリン代はいくらだ？」

「1ドル20セントです」

そのとき僕は、自分たちが誰かに見られている気配を感じた。修理工場の上を見上げると、窓からマートルがこっちを見下ろしていた。その表情が、驚きから怒りへ、怒りから何か別のものに変わっていった——嫉妬だろうか？ 僕はふと、彼女の見つめる先がトムではないのに気づいた。彼女はジョーダン・ベイカーを見ていた。彼女をトムの妻だと思い込んだのだ。

Daisy and Gatsby caught up to us on the road and we all ended up at the Plaza Hotel. We were all so tired and unhappy from the heat that hardly any of us knew what we were doing. We rented a hotel room with the idea that it would be cool. But sooner or later, we found ourselves in a room that was just as hot as being outside. We looked around unhappily at each other. Daisy went to the mirror and began fixing her hair.

"Open a window," she demanded.

"It's already open," said Jordan.

"Open another one."

"There aren't any more."

"We should forget the heat," cut in Tom. "You make it ten times worse, Daisy, by complaining about it all the time."

"Why don't you leave her alone, old sport?" said Gatsby. "You're the one who insisted we come to town."

There was a moment of silence.

"That's a great expression of yours, isn't it?" asked Tom with a mean smile on his face. "All this 'old sport' business. Where did you pick that up?"

"Now look here, Tom. If you're going to make personal remarks I'm not going to stay another minute," said Daisy. "Just call downstairs for some glasses and whiskey."

But Tom continued.

■catch up to ～に追いつく ■end up 最後は～に行き着く ■make ～ ten times worse ～を十倍も悪化させる ■all the time ひっきりなしに ■business 图 (軽蔑的に) 代物、事柄 ■Now look here ちょっと、あのですね ■make personal remark 人のことをとやかく言う

デイジーとギャツビーは途中で僕たちに追いつき、そろってプラザホテルに到着した。暑さのせいで誰もがくたびれて機嫌が悪く、自分たちが何をしているのかよくわからなくなっていた。僕たちは、そこなら涼しいだろう、という考えでホテルの部屋を取ることにした。ところが部屋に入ってまもなく、外と変わらないくらい暑いことに気づかされた。僕たちは不満げにお互いを見合った。デイジーは鏡の前に行って、髪を直しはじめた。

「窓を開けて」とデイジーは言った。

「もう開いてる」ジョーダンが答えた。

「他の窓を開けて」

「他の窓はないわ」

「暑いのは忘れよう」トムが口をはさんだ。「余計に暑く感じるだろう、デイジー。そうやって文句ばかり言うから」

「彼女の好きにさせてやらないか、きみ」ギャツビーが言った。「だいいち、街に来ようと言い張ったのはあなただ」

　一瞬、沈黙があった。

「ずいぶん大層な口癖じゃないか？」トムは意地悪く微笑んで言った。「その『きみ』って呼びかけだよ。どこで覚えたんだい？」

「ちょっと、トム。人のことをあれこれ言うんだったら、私はもう帰るわ」デイジーが言った。「電話して、グラスとウィスキーを持ってこさせてちょうだい」

　だがトムはやめなかった。

"I hear you're an Oxford man," he said, his eyes narrowing at Gatsby.

"I can't really say that, but I went there," said Gatsby.

"Oh, come on. Just admit to everybody you never went to Oxford. We all know it's a lie," said Tom.

"I did go there," said Gatsby. "It was 1919. I only stayed five months. That's why I can't really call myself an Oxford man."

Tom looked at all of us to see if we believed him. But we were all looking at Gatsby.

"It was an opportunity they gave to some of the officers after the war," Gatsby continued. "We could go to any of the universities in England or France."

So that was it! I was happy to find out that it was never a lie, that he had really gone to Oxford. But Tom was not finished.

"Well I have one more question for you, Mr. Gatsby. What kind of trouble are you trying to start in my house, anyway?"

We all held our breath. The secret was out in the open now.

"He isn't causing trouble," broke in Daisy. "You're causing trouble. Please have a little self-control."

"Self-control?" Tom exploded. "I suppose I should sit back and let Mr. Nobody from Nowhere make love to my wife. Well, that's never going to happen. I know I'm not very popular. I don't throw big parties. But I suppose you have to turn your house into a circus every Saturday to have any friends!"

■come on いい加減にしろ ■So that was it! そういうわけだったのか！ ■hold one's breath 固唾を呑む ■out in the open 公然と ■sit back 傍観する ■throw a party パーティーを開く ■turn ~ into a circus ～を大騒ぎにする

「オックスフォード出だと聞いているが」トムはギャツビーをねめつけた。

「正確にはそうとは言えませんが、行きました」ギャツビーは答えた。

「おいおい。もう認めたらどうだ。オックスフォードになど行っていないと。みんな嘘だと知ってるんだ」

「本当に行ったんです」ギャツビーは言った。「1919年に、5ヵ月間だけ在籍しました。ですから、オックスフォード出とまでは言えないのです」

トムは僕たちがこの言葉を信じたかどうかを見極めるようにみんなを見回した。でも、僕たちはギャツビーを見ていた。

「あれは戦争が終わった後、一部の将校に与えられた機会だったんです」ギャツビーはつづけた。「英国かフランスにあるどの大学にも行けるというものでした」

そうだったのか！ 決して嘘ではなかったとわかって、僕は嬉しかった。彼は本当にオックスフォードに行ったのだ。だがトムは黙らなかった。

「ではギャツビーさん、もう1つ聞きたいことがある。いったい僕の家でどういう面倒を起こすつもりなんだ？」

僕たちはみんな息を止めた。秘密がついに明るみに出てしまった。

「彼は面倒を起こしてなんかない」デイジーが割って入った。「面倒を起こしているのはあなたよ。少しは自分を抑えたらどうなの」

「自分を抑えるだと？」トムが大声で言った。「どこの馬の骨とも知れない男と自分の妻が寝ているのを黙って見ていろというのか。そうはいかないぞ。たしかに僕は、大して人気者ではない。派手なパーティーを開かないからな。だが友人を作りたければ、自宅で毎週末サーカスを開かなくてはいけないらしい！」

"I've got something to tell *you*, old sport—" began Gatsby. But Daisy cut in.

"Please don't!" she cried. "Let's all go home. Why don't we all go home?"

"That's a good idea," I said. "Come on, Tom. Nobody wants to stay here. Let's go."

"I want to know what Mr. Gatsby has to tell me."

"Your wife doesn't love you," said Gatsby. "She never loved you. She loves me."

"You must be crazy!" Tom shouted.

Gatsby jumped to his feet, shaking with excitement.

"She never loved you! She only married you because I was poor and she was tired of waiting for me. It was a terrible mistake but in her heart she never loved anyone but me!"

At this point Jordan and I tried to go, but Tom and Gatsby both insisted that we stay.

"That's a damn lie," said Tom. "Daisy loved me when she married me and she still does. And what's more, I love her too. Sometimes I make mistakes but I always come back, and in my heart I love her all the time."

"You're awful," said Daisy. She turned to me and said, "Do you know why we left Chicago? I'm surprised nobody has told you about *that* little mistake Tom made!"

---

■get something to tell ～に話がある ■jump to one's feet はじかれたように立ち上がる ■be tired of ～にうんざりする ■in one's heart 本音では ■damn lie ひどいうそ ■and what's more それに、さらに言えば

「きみ、言っておきたいことがある——」ギャツビーは言いかけたが、デイジーが割りこんだ。

「もうやめて！」デイジーは叫んだ。「帰りましょう。みんな帰りましょうよ」

「それがいい」僕は言った。「さあ、トム。誰もここにいたくないよ。行こう」

「ギャツビーさんが何を言いたいのか知りたい」

「奥さまはあなたを愛していません」ギャツビーは言った。「あなたを愛したことなどなかった。彼女は私を愛しています」

「頭がどうかしているのか！」トムは怒鳴った。

ギャツビーは立ち上がり、興奮に震えていた。

「彼女はあなたを愛したことなどない！ あなたと結婚したのは、私が貧しくて、私を待ちくたびれたからだ。それは大きな過ちだったが、彼女の心の中では、愛した男はこの私だけなんだ！」

僕とジョーダンは帰ろうとしたが、トムとギャツビーはみんな残るようにと譲らなかった。

「そんなのは嘘だ」トムは言った。「結婚したとき、デイジーは僕を愛していたし、今だってそうだ。何より、僕も彼女を愛している。ときには間違いをしでかすこともある。だがいつだって彼女のもとへ帰るし、心ではいつも彼女を愛している」

「あなたはひどいわ」デイジーは言った。そして僕の方を向いた。「どうして私たちがシカゴを離れたか知ってる？ トムのあのちょっとした過ちについて誰からも聞いてないとしたら驚きだわ！」

Gatsby walked over and stood beside her. "Daisy, that's all over now," he said. "It doesn't matter any more. Just tell him the truth—that you never loved him—and it will be done forever."

Daisy paused. Her eyes fell on Jordan and me as if she was asking us what she should do. It was as if she finally realized what she was doing, but she had never intended to do anything at all. But it was done now. It was too late.

"I never loved him," she said. But it didn't sound true.

"Not in France?" asked Tom suddenly.

"No."

"Not that day I carried you down from the Plaza to keep your shoes dry?" Tom's voice shook.... "Daisy?"

"Please don't," she said. Then she looked at Gatsby. "There, Jay, I said it!"

She tried to light a cigarette but her hand was shaking. Then she threw the cigarette on the floor and shouted at Gatsby, "You want too much! I love you now, isn't that enough? I can't help what has passed." She began to cry. "I did love him once. But I loved you too."

"You loved me *too*?" Gatsby repeated. His eyes were wide with shock.

■all over 終わって ■intend to 〜するつもりである ■carry 〜 down 〜を抱えて下りる ■there 副 ほら ■can't help what has passed 過ぎたことはどうしようもない

ギャツビーはデイジーの隣に歩み寄った。「デイジー、もう終わったんだ。そんなことは気にしなくていい。彼に本当のことを言ってくれ——愛したことは一度もなかったと——それですべてが終わる」

　デイジーは動かなかった。ジョーダンと僕の方を、どうすればいいかわからないという風に見つめた。まるで、自分が何をしていたかやっと気づき、そんなつもりではなかったと感じているかのようだった。だが、もう手遅れだった。

「彼を愛したことは一度もないわ」デイジーは言ったが、本心には聞こえなかった。

「フランスにいたときも？」トムがだしぬけに聞いた。

「ええ」

「靴が濡れないように、広場の丘からきみを抱きかかえて降りたときも？」トムの声が震えた。「デイジー？」

「お願い、やめて」デイジーは言った。そしてギャツビーを見た。「ほら、ジェイ、言ったわ！」

　デイジーは煙草に火をつけようとしたが、手が震えてできなかった。煙草を床に投げ捨てると、ギャツビーに叫んだ。「あなたは求めすぎよ！　私は今あなたを愛してる、それじゃ足りない？　過去はどうにもできないのよ！」彼女は泣きだした。「一度は彼を愛したの。でもあなたも愛していた」

「私も愛していた？」ギャツビーが繰り返した。衝撃に目を見開いていた。

"That's a lie!" shouted Tom. "She didn't even know you were alive. There are things between Daisy and me that you'll never know, things that neither of us can ever forget."

Tom's words seemed to bite physically into Gatsby.

"I can't say I never loved Tom," cried Daisy. "It wouldn't be true!"

"Of course it wouldn't," agreed Tom.

"As if it mattered to you!" she shouted at her husband.

"You don't understand," said Gatsby to Tom, "she's leaving you."

"She's not leaving me! Not for some dirty gangster like you! You'd have to steal the ring to put on her finger! Who are you, anyway? You're one of that group that hangs around Meyer Wolfsheim. I know that about you. But I'm going to find out more."

"That's fine," said Gatsby calmly.

"I found out what your 'medicine' stores were, too!" Tom turned to us and spoke rapidly. "He and this Wolfsheim character bought a lot of stores in poor neighborhoods. Then they sold illegal grain liquor there. And that's only one of his little tricks. I knew he was a criminal the first time I saw him!"

"So what?" said Gatsby. "One of your own friends, Walter Chase, did it too! But it's all right if one of your friends breaks the law, isn't it old sport?"

■bite into グサッと胸に突き刺さる ■As if it mattered to you! まるであなたに関係あるかのようね！（あなたには関係ない） ■That's fine. 構いませんよ。 ■grain liquor 穀物酒 ■break a law 法を破る

「それは嘘だ！」トムが叫んだ。「きみが生きているかどうかも彼女は知らなかったんだぞ。僕とデイジーのあいだには、きみにはわかりえないものがあるんだ。僕たちが永遠に忘れることのできないものが」

トムの言葉がギャツビーを本当に突き刺したかのように見えた。

「トムを愛したことがないなんて言えない」デイジーは泣いた。「だって本当じゃないもの！」

「もちろん、そうだろう」トムが頷いた。

「どうでもいいくせに！」デイジーは夫に叫んだ。

「わかってませんね」ギャツビーはトムに言った。「彼女はあなたと別れるつもりです」

「僕と別れるはずがない！ あんたみたいなろくでもないギャングのためにはな！ 彼女に贈る指輪だって、どうせ盗むに決まってる！ だいたい何者なんだ？ マイヤー・ウルフシャイムの取り巻きらしいな。それは知ってるんだ。だがもっと暴いてやるぞ」

「それは構いません」ギャツビーが穏やかに答えた。

「あのドラッグストアとやらの正体も調べたんだ！」トムは僕たちの方を振り向いて、早口でまくし立てた。「この男とウルフシャイムってやつが、貧しい地域にある店をいくつも買収したんだ。そしてそこで、密造酒を売っていた。だがそんなのは軽い悪事の1つにすぎない。僕はこの男を一目見たときから犯罪者だと思っていたよ！」

「だから何です？」ギャツビーは言った。「あなたのお友達のウォルター・チェイスだって同じでしょう。自分の友人なら法律を破っても構わないんですね、きみ？」

"Don't you call me 'old sport'!" cried Tom. "That 'medicine store' business was just small money for you. But now you've got some big deal going on with Wolfsheim that even Walter is too afraid to tell me about!"

Daisy's eyes looked to Tom and then to Gatsby in terror. Gatsby began to talk quickly to Daisy, telling her everything Tom said was untrue. But with every word, she was drawing further and further away from him.

"Oh, please, Tom!" she cried. "I can't stand this any more. Let's go home!"

"You and Mr. Gatsby go home in his car," said Tom. Daisy looked at him with fear in her eyes.

"It's all right, Daisy," Tom said in a slightly mean voice. "Mr. Gatsby won't bother you. I think he realizes all his tricks are over now."

Without a word, they left. All of a sudden, I realized something.

"I . . . I just remembered today is my birthday," I said.

I was thirty now. And stretching ahead of me was the dark, lonely road of a new decade.

At seven o'clock, Jordan, Tom, and I got into Tom's car and started driving home toward Long Island. All the way, Tom talked loudly and excitedly, knowing he had won.

■in terror おびえて　■draw away from 〜から離れていく　■over 既終わって　■all of a sudden 不意に　■stretch ahead 前方に広がっている　■all the way 最後までずっと

「『きみ』と呼ぶのはやめてくれ！」トムが叫んだ。「ドラッグストアの稼ぎはあんたにしたら小さなものだったんだろう。今またウルフシャイムと大きな計画を進めてるそうじゃないか。ウォルターでさえ怖がって僕に話せないほどのな！」

デイジーは怯えた目でトムを見、そしてギャツビーを見た。ギャツビーは、トムが言ったことはすべて嘘だとデイジーに慌てて言い聞かせた。だがギャツビーが何か言うたびに、彼女は彼からどんどん離れていった。

「お願いよ、トム！」彼女はわめいた。「もう耐えられない。早く帰りましょう！」

「きみはギャツビーさんと彼の車で帰るんだ」そう言われたデイジーは、恐ろしいものを見る目でトムを見た。

「気にするな、デイジー」トムはかすかにきつい声で言った。「ギャツビーさんはもうきみを困らせないだろう。小賢しいたくらみは終わったと気づいただろうからね」

ギャツビーとデイジーは、無言のまま部屋を出た。ふいに、僕はあることに気づいた。

「あの……いま思い出したんだけど、今日は僕の誕生日だ」僕は言った。

この日、僕は30歳になった。目の前には、暗く孤独な、新しい10年の道のりがのびていた。

午後7時に、ジョーダンとトムと僕は、トムの車でロングアイランドの家に向けて走り出した。車中、トムは興奮した様子でしゃべり通しだった。彼は自らの勝利を確信していた。

# 13

A young Greek man named Michaelis was the main witness of the accident. He lived across the street from Wilson's garage. At around five o'clock that evening, he went over to Wilson's and found him very sick in the office. Michaelis told him to go to bed, but Wilson refused. Then Michaelis heard yelling and a lot of noise coming from upstairs.

"I've got my wife locked in a room up there," Wilson said. "She's going to stay there until the day after tomorrow. Then I'm taking her away to the West."

Michaelis was shocked. He never thought Wilson was the type of man who could do such things. Michaelis asked why, but Wilson didn't explain. Instead, he looked at Michaelis with narrowed eyes and began asking where he was and what he was doing on certain days in the recent past. Michaelis began to feel uneasy and went home. But at around seven o'clock that evening, he heard Mrs. Wilson's voice shouting from across the street.

---

■live across the street from 〜と通りをはさんで向こう側に住む　■get someone locked in a room up（人）を部屋に閉じ込める　■feel uneasy 居心地悪さを感じる

# 13

　事故の主な目撃者は、ミカエリスという若いギリシャ人男性だった。ミカエリスはウィルソンの修理工場の向かいに住んでいた。その日の夕方5時頃、工場を訪ねると、ウィルソンが事務所でひどく具合悪そうにしていた。ベッドで休んだ方がいいと言ったが、ウィルソンは拒んだ。すると、2階からわめき声と激しい物音が聞こえた。

　「上の部屋に妻を閉じ込めているんだ」とウィルソンは言った。「明後日になったら出してやる。それで西部へ連れていくつもりだ」

　ミカエリスは驚いた。ウィルソンがそんなことをする男だとは思わなかったのだ。理由を尋ねたが、ウィルソンは答えなかった。そのかわり、ミカエリスを怪しむような目で見つめ、最近の何日かについて、どこで何をしていたのか聞きはじめた。ミカエリスは落ち着かない気持ちになり、家に帰った。しかしその日の7時頃、通りの向こうからウィルソンの怒鳴り声が聞こえてきた。

"Beat me, then!" she was yelling at Wilson. "Throw me down and beat me, or are you too afraid to?"

A moment later, she rushed out into the darkening night. She was waving her hands and shouting. But before Michaelis could do anything, it was all over.

The "death car," as the newspapers called it, didn't stop. It came out of the darkness then disappeared around the next bend in the road. Michaelis wasn't even sure of the car's color. At first he told the police that it was light green. The other car, the one heading toward New York, stopped a few feet down the road. The driver got out and ran back to where Myrtle Wilson lay bleeding in the middle of the road. Michaelis ran to her too. When they reached her, they knew she was already dead.

As Tom, Jordan, and I drove home, we saw a crowd and three or four cars gathered on the side of the road. Tom slowed down and didn't seem like he was going to stop until he realized that the crowd was in front of Wilson's garage. Then he looked worried and stopped the car.

"We'll just take a quick look," he said.

As we walked toward the garage, we heard someone repeating over and over, "Oh, my God! Oh, my God! Oh, my God!" There was a crowd gathered around something. Tom stretched to look over people's heads and suddenly made a strange noise in his throat.

---

■throw ~ down ～を投げ捨てる ■rush out 飛び出す ■wave one's hand 手を振る ■come out 現れる ■head toward ～に向かって進む ■take a look 見てみる

「それなら殴りなさいよ!」ウィルソンの妻が叫んでいた。「投げ倒して殴りなさいよ。それとも怖くてできないの?」
　一瞬ののち、夕闇の中を彼女が飛び出してきた。両手を振りまわし、何かを叫んでいた。だがミカエリスがどうすることもできないうちに、すべては終わった。
　「死の車」と新聞が名づけた車は止まらなかった。暗闇から現れたかと思うと、次の角を曲がって消え去った。ミカエリスは車の色さえはっきりわからなかった。最初、警察には薄い緑色だったと答えた。ニューヨークに向かって走っていたもう1台の車が、少し先で止まった。運転していた人が降りてきて、道の真ん中で血を流して倒れているマートル・ウィルソンのところへ駆けもどった。ミカエリスも駆けつけた。そばまで行くと、彼女がもう死んでいるのがわかった。

　トムとジョーダンと僕が車で家へ帰る途中、道の脇に人垣ができて、3、4台の車が止まっているのが見えた。トムはスピードを落としたが、止まる気はなさそうだった。だが、そこがウィルソンの店の前だと気がつくと、心配そうな顔をして車を止めた。

　「ちょっと様子を見てこよう」トムは言った。
　店に近づくと、誰かが「ああ、なんてことだ! なんてことだ!」と繰り返し叫ぶ声が聞こえた。何かを囲んで人だかりができていた。トムは首をのばして人々の頭越しにのぞきこんだ。突然、彼ののどが奇妙な音をたてた。

Then he pushed people out of his way and moved toward the center of the crowd.

Myrtle Wilson's body lay on a table. She was wrapped in two blankets. Tom went to her side and just stood there, staring. I realized the person yelling "Oh, my God!" was Wilson. He stood to the side of the garage, in the doorway to his office. He rocked back and forth, staring at his wife's body, weeping and repeating those three words. A man was at his side, trying to speak softly to him.

Tom turned to a policeman taking notes. "Hey," he said roughly, "what happened here? I need to know!"

"A car hit her. She was instantly killed."

"Instantly killed?" repeated Tom, staring.

"She ran out in the road. The driver didn't even stop his car."

"There were two cars," said Michaelis, "going opposite ways. One was coming from New York and the other was going. She ran out there and the one coming from New York knocked right into her, going thirty or forty miles an hour."

Another man stepped forward. "It was a big yellow car," he said.

"Did you see the accident?" asked the policeman.

"No, but the car passed me down the road, going much faster than forty miles an hour. Maybe fifty or sixty."

■body 名遺体　■rock back and forth 前後に揺れる　■take a note メモを取る　■be instantly killed 即死する　■knock into ～にぶつかる　■step forward 進み出る

トムは人を押しのけて、人だかりの中心に進んでいった。

　作業台の上に、マートル・ウィルソンの死体が横たわっていた。彼女は2枚の毛布に包まれていた。トムはそのかたわらに行き、立ちつくして見つめた。「ああ、なんてことだ！」と叫んでいたのはウィルソンだと僕は気づいた。彼は修理工場のわきの事務所の戸口に立っていた。前後に体を揺らしながら、妻の姿を見つめ、涙を流して同じ言葉を繰り返していた。1人の男が隣にいて、優しく声をかけようとしていた。

　トムは聞き取りをしている警官に話しかけた。「おい」トムは粗い口調で言った。「何があった？　教えてくれ！」
「彼女が車にひかれたんだ。即死だ」
「即死？」トムは目を見開いて繰り返した。
「彼女が道路に飛び出した。車は止まりもしなかったそうだ」
「2台の車がいたんです」ミカエリスが言った。「ニューヨーク側から来る車と、ニューヨークへ向かう車と。彼女が飛び出して、ニューヨークからきた車が彼女を正面からはねました。時速30マイルか40マイルは出てましたね」
　別の男が進み出て言った。「あれは大きな黄色い車でした」

「事故を見たのかね？」警官は聞いた。
「いいえ、でも少し先で、その車が僕の横を走り去っていったんです。時速40マイルどころか、5、60マイルは出ていたと思います」

Suddenly, Wilson yelled out to the crowd. He had heard part of this conversation.

"You don't have to tell me what kind of car it was! I know it! I saw it today!" he cried out. Tom got very stiff, and after a moment, he walked over to Wilson. He took the thin man by his shoulders and began talking to him in a low voice.

"Listen, I just got here a minute ago from New York," he said. "I was bringing you my car that you wanted to buy from me. That yellow car I was driving this afternoon wasn't mine. Do you understand me? I haven't seen it all afternoon."

Wilson just stared at him. Tom picked up Wilson as lightly as if he were a doll, and carried him into the office. He sat him down in a chair and came back out.

"Somebody ought to sit with him and watch him," he said to the crowd. Then he turned to me and said, "Let's go."

After Jordan, Tom, and I were back in the car, Tom drove slowly at first, then drove faster and faster. He began to cry. "He didn't even stop his car!" he said.

When we reached Tom's house, we saw there were several lights on.

"Daisy's home," he said, and we all got out of the car. As we walked toward the house, Tom invited us to have some supper and offered to call me a taxi to take me home.

■yell out to ～を大声で呼ぶ ■get stiff 硬直する ■take ～ by the shoulders ～の両肩をつかむ ■sit ～ down ～を座らせる

そのとき、ウィルソンが人だかりの中から声を張り上げた。今の会話が耳に入ったのだ。
「どんな車かなんて聞かなくてもわかる！　私は知ってるんだ！　今日、それを見たんだから！」ウィルソンは叫んだ。トムは一瞬からだを強張らせ、やがてウィルソンに歩み寄った。痩せこけた男の肩をつかみ、低い声で話しはじめた。
「いいかい、僕はニューヨークからたった今ここに着いた」トムは言った。「きみが買いたがっている車を持ってきたところなんだ。午後に乗っていたあの黄色い車は僕のものじゃない。わかったね？　あれからあの車はずっと見てないんだ」
　ウィルソンはただトムを見つめるだけだった。トムはウィルソンを人形のように軽々と抱き上げて事務所に入り、椅子に座らせてから外へ出てきた。
「誰か彼のそばに座って様子を見てやってくれ」トムは人だかりに向かって言った。そして僕の方に振り向いた。「さあ、行こう」
　ジョーダンと僕が乗り込んだ後、トムははじめゆっくり車を走らせ、それから一気にスピードを上げていった。そして泣きはじめた。「あいつ、車を止めもしなかったなんて！」
　トムの家に着くと、灯りがいくつかともっていた。

「デイジーが帰っている」トムはそう言って、僕たちはみんな車を降りた。家の方へ歩きながら、トムは軽い夕食をとっていくようすすめ、僕に帰りのタクシーを呼ぼうと言った。

"I don't want any food right now," I said. "I'll just stay out here and wait for the taxi."

I was feeling a little sick and I wanted to be alone. I didn't even want to be with Jordan.

"It's only nine-thirty," said Jordan. But I had had enough of all of them, and something in my face must have told her so. She looked hurt, and then quickly turned and walked into the house. When they had all gone, I sat down on the steps with my head in my hands. Then I heard footsteps coming toward me. When I looked up, I saw Gatsby, half hidden in the darkness.

"What are you doing?" I asked.

"Just standing here, old sport."

I was sick of him too. I wanted to go home.

"Did you see any trouble on the road?" he asked after a minute.

"Yes."

He paused.

"Was she killed?"

"Yes."

"I thought so. I told Daisy I thought so. But she didn't want to stop. I think she was too shocked. I got us back to West Egg on a smaller side road and hid the car in my garage," he said. "Who was the woman?"

■feel sick 気分が悪い　■have enough もうたくさんである　■be sick of ～にうんざりしている　■get ~ back to … ～を…へ戻す

「今は何も食べたくない」と僕は言った。「家の外でタクシーを待たせてもらえればいいよ」

少し気分が悪くて、1人きりになりたかった。ジョーダンとさえ一緒にいたくなかった。

「まだ9時半よ」ジョーダンは言った。でも、みんなにうんざりしている気持ちが僕の顔に出ていたのだろう。彼女は傷ついたような顔をして、さっと背を向けて家の中に入っていった。2人がいなくなると、僕はポーチの階段に座り、両手で頭を抱えた。すると、足音が僕の方に近づいてきた。顔を上げると、闇にまぎれてギャツビーが目の前にいた。

「いったい何をしてるんだ？」僕は聞いた。
「ただここに立っているんですよ、きみ」
僕は彼にもうんざりしていた。家に帰りたかった。
「途中で何か騒ぎを見かけましたか？」ややあってギャツビーが聞いた。
「ああ」
彼は一瞬黙った。
「彼女は死んだのですか？」
「ああ」
「そう思いました。デイジーにもそう言ったんです。でも彼女は止まろうとしなかった。きっとショックが大きすぎたんでしょう。ウェスト・エッグまで裏道で帰って、車は私のガレージに隠しました。それで、あの女は誰だったんですか？」

"Her name was Myrtle Wilson. Her husband owns the garage there. How the hell did it happen?" I demanded. I disliked him so much now.

"Well, I tried to swing the wheel..." He didn't finish, and suddenly I guessed at the truth.

"Was Daisy driving?"

"Yes," he said. "But of course I'll say I was driving if anybody asks. You see, when we left New York she was feeling very bad and she thought it would calm her if she drove. And this woman just rushed into the road out of nowhere... We were about to pass another car coming the other way. It all happened in a moment, but it seemed like she was coming toward us to speak to us. First, Daisy turned away from the woman toward the other car, but then she was afraid of hitting the car and turned back. The second my hand reached the wheel, we had hit her... It must have killed her instantly."

"It ripped her open—"

"Don't tell me, old sport." His face looked pained. "Well, Daisy just sped up. I tried to make her stop, but she just couldn't. I finally made her, and she just fell over into my lap. Then I drove us to my house. I think she'll be all right tomorrow," he said, looking up at the windows. "I'm just going to wait here and see if Tom tries to bother her. She locked herself in her room. If he tries to hurt her, she's going to turn the light off and then on again, so I'll know."

■how the hell 一体全体どうやって ■feel bad 気を悪くする ■out of nowhere どこからともなく ■turn away そらせる ■rip ~ open ~を裂いて開く ■see if ~ かどうか確かめる ■lock oneself in ~に閉じこもる

「名前はマートル・ウィルソン。夫はあそこの修理工場の主人だ。何であんなことになった？」僕は問いつめた。ギャツビーがたまらなく嫌いになっていた。

「その、何とかハンドルを取ろうとしたんですが……」ギャツビーが口ごもり、僕はふいに真相を察した。

「デイジーが運転していたのか？」

「ああ」ギャツビーは言った。「もちろん、もし聞かれたら自分が運転していたと答えるつもりです。ほら、ニューヨークを出たとき、彼女はだいぶ動揺していたから、運転すれば落ち着くと思ったみたいなんです。そこへ、あの女がどこからともなく飛び出してきた……。向こうから来る車とすれ違おうとするところだったんです。すべてが一瞬の出来事でしたが、彼女は何かを伝えにきたようにも見えました。最初、デイジーは女をよけようと対向車の方にハンドルを切ったんですが、車にぶつかるのが怖くて元に戻しました。次に私がハンドルを取ろうとしたときには、もう女をはねていたんです……即死だったに違いありません」

「体が裂けて——」

「それは言わないでください、きみ」ギャツビーは顔をゆがめた。「それから、デイジーはスピードを上げました。止まらせようとしたけど、彼女には無理でした。やっと止まったと思ったら、私の膝に倒れ込んでしまいました。その後は私が運転して家まで帰りました。彼女も明日には落ち着くでしょう」ギャツビーは窓を見上げて言った。「私はここに残って、トムが彼女を追い詰めたりしないか見張るつもりです。彼女は自室に鍵をかけてこもっています。もしトムが手荒な真似をすれば、部屋の灯りを点滅させて知らせてくれることになっているんです」

"He won't touch her," I said.

"I don't trust him, old sport."

"How long are you going to wait?"

"All night, if necessary."

"You wait here," I said. "I'll take a look around."

I walked back toward the kitchen softly, and looked up into the window. I saw Daisy and Tom sitting at the kitchen table, facing each other. There was a plate of cold chicken between them, and two bottles of beer. He was talking to her, and sometimes she would look up at him and nod.

They weren't happy, but they weren't unhappy either. There was definitely the feeling of a man and his wife planning something together.

I walked quietly back toward Gatsby. He was waiting for me.

"Is it all quiet up there?" he asked anxiously.

"Yes, it's all quiet." I added, "You better come home and get some sleep."

He shook his head.

"I want to wait here until Daisy goes to bed. Good night, old sport."

Then he turned back to the house eagerly, as if he didn't want me to bother him as he watched the house. So I walked away and left him standing there—watching over nothing.

■take a look around 辺りを見回す ■face each other お互い向き合う ■up there あそこで ■better do ～したほうがよい

「トムは手を上げたりしないよ」僕は言った。
「私は彼を信用していないんです、きみ」
「いつまでここで待つつもりだ？」
「必要なら、一晩中でも」
「ここにいてくれ」僕は言った。「ちょっと様子を見てくる」

僕はキッチンの方へそっと引き返し、窓の中をのぞいた。デイジーとトムが、キッチンのテーブルに向い合って座っていた。2人のあいだには、冷めたチキンを乗せた皿が1枚と、ビールの瓶が2本置いてあった。トムが彼女に話しかけ、彼女がときおり顔を上げ、彼の顔を見て頷く。

2人は幸せに見えなかった。でも、不幸せにも見えなかった。ともに何かを企てる男とその妻の雰囲気が、まぎれもなく感じられた。

僕は足音を立てずにギャツビーのもとへ戻った。彼は僕を待っていた。
「向こうは静かでしたか？」彼は不安そうに聞いた。
「ああ、すごく静かだった」僕はこう言い添えた。「きみも家に帰って少し休んだ方がいい」
ギャツビーは首を横に振った。
「デイジーがベッドに入るまで待ちたい。お休みなさい、きみ」

ギャツビーはそう言って、足早に家の方へ戻っていった。まるで、見張っている間は僕に邪魔されたくないみたいだった。だから僕はギャツビーを残してその場をあとにした。むなしい見張りに立つ彼を残して。

# 覚えておきたい英語表現

> In that little moment, Daisy had silently told Gatsby that she loved him, ... (p.146, 下から4行目)
> そのほんの一瞬で、デイジーは静かにギャツビーに愛を告げたのだ……

【解説】silentlyを英英辞典で引いてみると、"without speaking（口に出さずに）"とか "without using words or sounds to express something（何かを表現するのに言葉や音を使わないこと）" という説明がなされています。周囲に人などいないかのように見つめ合ったギャツビーとデイジー。デイジーはなんとか視線をギャツビーから引き離して再び言いました。

> You always look so cool.　あなたはいつだって涼しげね。

同じ部屋にいるニックやトムには、デイジーが "I love you, Jay." と言っているも同然だとあからさまに伝わっています。デイジーがどのような表情で、言い方で、声色で、この言葉を言っているのかを想像してみてください。

> She's been fooling around with some other man around here. (p.152, 9行目)
> 女房はこの近辺にいる他の男と浮気し続けてきたんですよ。

【解説】fool around with〜 で「〜と浮気する」という意味です。foolは「馬鹿な」という意味から、「〜と馬鹿げた何かしらをする」という直訳になるでしょうか。
ウィルソンは、"She's been fooling." と現在完了進行形（have+been+Ving）を用いていますから、妻マートルの不倫が現在も進行中であることに気付いています。だから出発までマートルを部屋に閉じ込めているのでしょう。
上流階級出身ゆえ、他人への思いやりに欠けるトムは、次の瞬間にはそそくさと会計を済ませようとしています。反省している素振りは全くありませんね。

> Where did you pick that up?（p.154, 18行目）
> 一体、どこでそんな言葉を拾ったんだ？

**【解説】**プラザホテルでデイジーを巡り口喧嘩を始めたトムが、男性への呼称として"old sport"を使うギャツビーを罵った言葉です。"pick 〜 up"で「〜を拾う」です。代々金持ちの家に生まれたトムは、いわゆる成金であるギャツビーを軽蔑しています。デイジーに釣り合う男になるために、上流階級らしく振る舞っているギャツビーを痛烈に皮肉った言葉がこの台詞です。

> Daisy turned away from the woman toward the other car, but then she was afraid of hitting the car and turned back.
> （p.176, 13行目）
> デイジーはその女性を避けて対向車の方にハンドルを切ったのですが、車に衝突するのが怖くなり元の車線に戻ったんです。

**【解説】**be afraid of Vingで「Vすることを恐れる」です。デイジーは「女性を轢く＝自分は多分助かる」と「対向車とぶつかる＝女性は助かるが自分はタダでは済まない」を瞬間的に天秤にかけ、マートルを轢いて自分は助かる方を選択します。

　トム同様、生まれながらの上流階級であるデイジーは、他人の命よりも我が身の保全の方が大事だったのです。これはこの後、話の結末に向け大事な伏線になってきます。

> So I walked away and left him standing there—watching over nothing.（p.178, 下から2行目）
> だから僕は歩き出した——何も起きようのないものを見守って立ち続ける彼をそこに残して。

**【解説】**leave A Bで「AをBのままにして去る」という意味です。standingは現在分詞です。watch overは「見守る」とか「見張る」という意味です。ギャツビーは

我が身を省みず、デイジーのことを心配すると同時に、「何か起こること」を期待しています。デイジーを助け出し連れ去るためでしょう。

　しかし、キッチンで向かい合うトムとデイジーを見たニックは、"nothing"と断言します。nothingは「何もない」ですから、ギャツビーが心配しつつも期待していることが「何も起きるはずがない」と言っているのです。悲しいほどピュアで一途なギャツビーの姿が、読者に結末を予想させるようで胸が痛みます。

# Part 5

# 14

I couldn't sleep all night. I had terrible dreams and kept waking up. Sometime toward dawn, I heard a taxi go up Gatsby's road, and I knew he was returning from Daisy's house. I got up, got dressed, and walked over.

Gatsby saw me coming across his yard. He looked tired.

"Nothing happened," he said. "I waited, and at about four o'clock she came to the window and stood there for a minute and then turned out the light."

His house was huge, but it never seemed bigger than that morning. We walked from room to room, looking for cigarettes. When we finally found some, we went outside and smoked silently.

"You ought to go away," I finally said.

"Go away *now*, old sport?" He wouldn't hear of it. He couldn't possibly leave Daisy now. He was holding onto some last hope and I couldn't bear to shake him free.

---

■go up ～に近づく　■come across ～を渡って来る　■hold onto ～にしがみつく
■can't bear to ～するに忍びない　■shake ～ free ～を振りほどく

# 14

 一晩中眠れなかった。何度も恐ろしい夢を見ては、目を覚ました。夜明け近く、ギャツビー邸の私道にタクシーが入ってくる音がして、彼がデイジーの家から帰ってきたのがわかった。僕は起きて服を着ると、彼のところへ行った。
 ギャツビーは邸宅の庭を歩いてくる僕に気づいた。彼は疲れているようだった。
「何ごともなかった」彼は言った。「待っていたら、4時頃彼女が窓際に現われて、しばらくそこに立っていた後、灯りを消した」
 彼の家は広大だったが、あの朝ほど広く感じたことはなかった。僕たちは部屋から部屋へ、煙草を探して歩いた。やっと何本か見つけると、外へ出て何も言わずに煙草を吸った。

「きみはここを離れた方がいい」僕はついに口を開いた。
「今すぐ行けというんですか、きみ？」ギャツビーは聞き入れそうもなかった。デイジーのそばを離れるなんて、このときの彼にはできなかっただろう。残された最後の希望にしがみつく彼を引きはがすことは僕にもできなかった。

It was this morning that he told me about Dan Cody and his past. He also told me how he met Daisy. He was a young officer in the army, about to be sent to Europe for the war. Before he went, he was stationed at Camp Taylor, in Louisville, for a month. He went over to Daisy's house one day with a group of other invited officers. Her house was the most beautiful house he had ever seen, and he remembered walking through it in wonder.

When he met Daisy, the first thing he noticed was her voice. He heard so much *money* in it. It was a rich voice—the voice of a lovely girl who had grown up in a lovely house, whose whole life had been lovely. It was a mystery to him, and he wanted to know more.

Gatsby was surprised when he fell in love with Daisy. And he was surprised when she fell in love with him too. He knew things that she didn't know because of all his travels and experiences. He had such great dreams and plans for his future. But telling Daisy about all the things he planned to do was suddenly more fun than actually doing them. Right then and there, he decided to give his plans, his dreams, and his life to Daisy.

■station 動配備する　■fall in love with ～と恋に落ちる　■right then and there その瞬間にその場で

ギャツビーがダン・コーディーと自分の過去について打ち明けてくれたのは、この朝のことだった。デイジーとの出会いについても話してくれた。当時ギャツビーは陸軍の若い将校で、ヨーロッパの戦地に送られようとしていた。出征前の1ヵ月間を過ごしたのが、ルイヴィルにあるテイラー基地だった。ギャツビーはある日、仲間の将校たちとともにデイジーの家に招かれた。彼女の家は、かつて彼が見たどんな家よりも美しかった。そこへ足を踏み入れたときの驚きは忘れないという。

　デイジーに初めて会ったとき、まず印象に残ったのは声だった。その声から、ありあまる富が聞きとれた。豊かな声──美しい家で育ち、人生すべてが美しい、美しい娘の声。それは彼にとって神秘であり、もっとよく知りたいと思った。

　自分がデイジーに恋をしたことにギャツビーは驚いた。そしてデイジーが自分に恋をしたことにも驚いた。デイジーにとってギャツビーは、旅やさまざまな経験から自分の知らないことを知っている存在だった。彼には将来に向けて大きな夢や構想もあった。ところが突然、そうした計画をデイジーに語ることの方が、じっさいに達成することよりも楽しくなった。たちまち彼は、夢も計画も人生も、すべてデイジーに捧げようと決めたのだ。

On the night before he went to Europe, he sat with Daisy in his arms for a long time. They didn't say much, but they touched each other's hands, and once he kissed her dark shining hair. They told each other without words how much they loved each other.

He did very well in the war, but all he wanted to do after the war was to go back home. However, the army made a mistake and sent him to Oxford instead. He started to get worried. Daisy's letters to him were starting to sound as if she were giving up on waiting. She couldn't understand why he couldn't come home. Meanwhile, life went on for Daisy. As much as she missed Gatsby, there were still parties for her to go to, young men to dance with, friends who still expected to see her every evening. She simply couldn't stop the passing of time.

Then, in the middle of spring, Tom Buchanan came along. There was something so solid and reassuring about him. Gatsby could only offer her promises, while Tom offered her reality. After the wedding, Daisy wrote to Gatsby. Her letter reached him while he was still at Oxford.

When Gatsby returned from Oxford, he made one last visit to Louisville just to walk down the same streets he and Daisy used to walk down together. Then he went to New York to make his fortune.

■do well in 〜で活躍する　■get worried 心配になる　■give up on 〜に見切りをつける　■come along 現れる　■make one's fortune 財産を築く

ヨーロッパへ発つ前夜、ギャツビーはデイジーを腕に抱いて長い間座っていた。2人の口数は少なかったが、互いに手を触れあい、ギャツビーは彼女の黒く艶やかな髪に一度口づけた。2人は何も言わずに、どんなに愛しているかを伝えあった。

　ギャツビーは戦争で活躍したが、彼の望みは戦争が終わったら一刻も早く帰国することだった。ところが軍の手違いで、オックスフォード大学に送られてしまった。彼は不安になりはじめた。デイジーからの手紙には、これ以上待てないというあきらめが滲みはじめていた。デイジーはどうして彼が帰ってこられないのか、理解できなかった。そんな中、彼女の人生も動いていった。ギャツビーを想いながらも、相変わらずパーティーはあるし、一緒に踊る若い男たちや、毎晩彼女に会うのを楽しみにしている友達もいた。彼女には時の流れを止めることはできなかった。

　そして春の盛りに、トム・ブキャナンが現れた。その姿にはどこか揺るぎなさと安心感があった。ギャツビーがデイジーに与えるのは約束だけだったが、トムは現実を与えてくれた。結婚式の後、デイジーはギャツビーに手紙を書いた。手紙は、彼がまだオックスフォードにいる間に届いた。

　オックスフォードから帰ってきたギャツビーは、最後にもう一度ルイヴィルを訪ね、デイジーとともに歩いた道をひとり歩いた。その後ニューヨークへ財産を築くために発った。

It was around nine o'clock in the morning when Gatsby finished telling me this. We had breakfast, then we went outside. The weather was now mild—it would be another warm, late summer day. The gardener told Gatsby he would empty the pool that day.

"The leaves will start falling soon, sir," the gardener said. "We should empty the pool if we don't want any trouble with the pipes."

"Don't do it today," said Gatsby. He turned to me and said, "You know, old sport, I haven't used that pool all summer. Shall we go for a swim?"

I wanted to say yes. For some strange reason, I did not want to leave him alone. But it was past nine now and I had to take the train to work.

"I can't," I said. "But I'll call you today around noon."

"Do, old sport."

We shook hands and I walked away. But just before I reached the edge of his yard, I turned around.

"They're a bad crowd," I yelled at him across the lawn. "You're worth more than the whole bunch of them!"

I've always been glad I said that. It was the only praise I ever gave him. First he nodded politely, then his face broke into that beautiful, understanding smile of his.

"Goodbye," I called. "I enjoyed breakfast, Gatsby."

---

■empty a pool プールの水を抜く　■yell at ～に向かって叫ぶ　■whole bunch of 非常にたくさんの　■break into smile 突然笑顔になる

ギャツビーがすべてを話し終えたのは、朝の9時頃だった。僕たちは朝食をとり、それから外へ出た。天気は穏やかだった——また、夏の終わりの暖かな一日になりそうだった。庭師がギャツビーに、今日プールの水を抜こうと思います、と声をかけた。
「そろそろ葉が落ちはじめます」庭師は言った。「配管が詰まると面倒ですので、水を抜いてしまった方がよいかと」

「今日はやめてくれ」ギャツビーは言った。そして僕の方を向いた。「実はね、きみ、この夏は一度もプールに入ってないんだ。一緒に泳ぎませんか？」
　僕はそうしようと言いたかった。なぜだかわからないが、彼を1人にしておきたくなかったのだ。でも時間は9時を過ぎていて、電車で仕事に行かなくてはならなかった。
「無理そうだ」僕は言った。「でも、昼頃電話をするよ」
「そうしてください、きみ」
　ギャツビーと握手をして、僕は歩きだした。でも庭の端まできたところで、振り返った。
「みんなろくでもない連中だ」僕は芝生の向こうのギャツビーに叫んだ。「あいつらをひとまとめにしたって、きみの価値には及ばないよ！」
　そう言ってよかったと、今でも思っている。あれは僕が彼に伝えた唯一の賛辞だった。ギャツビーはまず礼儀正しく頷き、それから、あの美しく思いやりのある微笑みを弾けさせた。
「さようなら」僕は大きな声で言った。「朝食をありがとう、ギャツビー」

# 15

Up in the city, I tried to do some work, but I fell asleep in my chair instead. The ringing telephone woke me up at around noon. It was Jordan Baker.

"I left Daisy's house," she said. "I'm at Hempstead now. You weren't so nice to me last night."

I knew she was right. But the truth was, I didn't really care.

"How could it have mattered?" I asked.

She was silent for a moment. Then she said, "However, I want to see you." She asked if we could meet that day, but I said no, I was busy. There was no gladness in our words or voices. But we set a date to meet, and we both hung up the phone sharply.

I called Gatsby's house a few minutes later, but the line was busy. I tried four times, but each time, I couldn't get through. I decided to go home early, on the 3:50 p.m. train.

■up in the city 街にいて　■Hempstead 図ヘムステッド《地名》　■nice to 〜に親切にする　■set a date 日取りを決める　■hang up 電話を切る　■a line is busy 話中である　■get through 連絡がつく

# 15

　ニューヨークに着いて、仕事に手をつけようとしたけれど、椅子に座ったまま眠ってしまった。昼頃、電話のベルで起こされた。ジョーダン・ベイカーからだった。
　「デイジーの家を出たの。今はヘムステッドにいる。あなた、昨夜は私に冷たかったわね」
　彼女の言う通りなのはわかっていた。でも正直なところ、どうでもよかった。
　「それどころじゃなかっただろう？」僕は言った。
　一瞬黙りこんでから彼女は言った。「そうだけど、あなたに会いたいの」
　これから会えないかと聞かれたが、忙しいから無理だと答えた。僕たちの言葉にも声にも、嬉しさはまるでなかった。それでも会う日時を決め、お互いに電話を叩きつけるように切った。
　数分してからギャツビーの家に電話をかけたが、話し中だった。4回ためしたが、いずれもつながらなかった。僕は午後3時50分の電車で早く帰ることにした。

As I rode the train home, I looked out the window into the land of dust to see if there was still a crowd around Wilson's garage. I was surprised to find nobody there. Later on, I found out what happened after Tom, Jordan, and I left the sad scene the night before.

Myrtle's sister, Catherine, was called. She arrived after the body had been moved to a hospital. Some kind or curious person drove her there. After the police and the crowd had left, Michaelis sat with Wilson in the little office. Wilson didn't sleep through the night. He stared at the wall and would sometimes cry out, "Oh, my god!"

Toward dawn, Wilson started saying strange things to Michaelis.

"I can find out whose yellow car that was," he whispered. Then he told Michaelis that a couple of months ago, his wife had come home with a broken nose. He then told Michaelis to open the top drawer of a desk in the office. When Michaelis opened it, he found a black leather dog leash.

"This? It's just a dog leash," said Michaelis.

Wilson stared and nodded.

"I found it yesterday. It was wrapped up in nice paper," said Wilson. He started rocking from side to side. "Then he killed her."

"Who did?"

---

■ride a train home 帰りの電車に乗る ■later on 後になって ■dawn 图夜明け
■wrap up 包む ■from side to side 左右に

家に向かう電車の窓から灰の一帯を眺め、ウィルソンの店の周りにまだ人が集まっているかどうか見ようと思った。驚いたことに、そこには誰もいなかった。昨日の夜、トムとジョーダンと僕が悲しい現場を去ってから起きたことを、僕は後になって知った。

　まず、マートルの妹のキャサリンが呼び出された。彼女が着いたのは、マートルの遺体が病院に運ばれた後だった。親切かあるいは物好きな誰かが、彼女を車に乗せて病院へ連れていった。警察と見物人がいなくなった後、ミカエリスは狭い事務所でウィルソンに付き添った。ウィルソンは朝まで一睡もせず、壁を見つめ、ときおり「なんてことだ！」と叫んだ。

　夜明け近くに、ウィルソンはミカエリスにわけのわからないことを言い出した。
　「あの黄色い車が誰のものかは調べられるんだ」と彼はつぶやいた。そしてミカエリスに、2ヵ月前、妻が鼻をけがして帰ってきたことがあったことを話すと、事務所の机の一番上の引き出しを開けるように言った。ミカエリスが開けて見ると、犬用の黒い革紐が入っていた。

　「これかい？　ただの犬の散歩紐じゃないか」ミカエリスは言った。
　ウィルソンはじっと見て頷いた。
　「昨日見つけたんだ。きれいな包装紙に包んであった」ウィルソンはそう言って、体を揺すりはじめた。「あげくにやつは妻を殺したんだ」
　「誰が？」

"I'll find out," said Wilson.

"You're not making any sense," Michaelis said. "You're tired, George. Why don't you lay down here and try to get some sleep?"

"He killed her!"

"It was an accident, George," Michaelis said.

George Wilson shook his head. "I know!" he said. "It was the man in that car. She ran out to speak to him and he wouldn't stop." Wilson's eyes turned toward the window, and he walked over to it. He leaned his head against the glass and said, "I told her. I told her she might trick me, but she couldn't trick God. I brought her here, to this window, and I showed her. I said, 'Look! God knows what you've been doing—everything you've been doing. You can't trick God!'"

Michaelis stared at Wilson, then joined him at the window. He realized with shock that Wilson was looking at the huge eyes of Doctor T. J. Eckleburg.

"That's just an advertisement, George," he said softly.

"God sees everything," repeated Wilson.

By 6 a.m. Michaelis was too tired to stay awake. He told Wilson he would be right across the street if he needed anything. Then he went home and went to sleep. Four hours later, Michaelis woke up and went over to Wilson's to check on him. But Wilson was gone.

■not make sense 意味をなさない　■Why don't you ~ ? ~したらどうですか？　■stay awake 起きている　■check on ~を点検する

「見つけてみせる」ウィルソンは言った。

「何を言ってるんだかまるでわからないよ」ミカエリスは言った。「疲れているんだ、ジョージ。ここで横になって少し寝たらどうだ？」

「やつが殺したんだ！」

「あれは事故だったんだよ、ジョージ」ミカエリスは言った。

ジョージ・ウィルソンは首を横に振った。「わかってるんだ！」彼は言った。「あの車に乗っていたあの男だ。妻は話しかけようと駆け寄ったが、あの男は止まろうともしなかった」ウィルソンは窓の方に目を向け、歩いていった。そして窓ガラスに頭をもたせかけて言った。「妻に言ったんだ。俺をだませても、神様はだませないと。ここに、この窓辺に連れてきて見せてやったよ。『見てみろ！　神様はお前のやっていることをお見通しだ──何もかもお見通しだ！　神様をだますことはできない！』とな」

ミカエリスはウィルソンをじっと見つめ、窓辺に行って傍らに立った。ウィルソンの見ているものがT・J・エックルバーグ博士の巨大な目だと気づいて、ミカエリスはぞっとした。

「あれはただの看板だよ、ジョージ」ミカエリスは優しく言った。

「神様はすべてお見通しだ」ウィルソンは繰り返した。

朝の6時にもなると、ミカエリスもくたびれて起きているのが辛くなった。ウィルソンに、何かあれば通りの向かいにいるからと伝え、家に帰って眠りについた。4時間後に目を覚まし、ウィルソンの様子を見にいった。しかし彼の姿はなくなっていた。

Later, the police were able to trace George Wilson's movement from the garage to Port Roosevelt, and then to Gad's Hill. He was on foot the whole time. At Gad's Hill he had bought a sandwich that he didn't eat. Some boys had seen him walking down the road. They told the police that he was "acting kind of crazy." By about 2:30 p.m., he was in West Egg. He asked someone the way to Gatsby's house. So by that time, he knew Gatsby's name.

At two o'clock, Gatsby put on his swimming suit and headed out to the pool. He had kept his telephone line open in case Daisy called, and that was why I couldn't get through to him. But Daisy never called. Perhaps he knew she wouldn't. And perhaps he no longer cared. I believe he went out to the pool that day feeling that he had lost his old, warm world. He had lived too long with a single dream, and now he was paying the price. He must have looked up at the sky and seen a world he didn't recognize.

One of the servants heard the shots, but he said he didn't realize what the sounds were. When I came rushing to Gatsby's house shortly afterward, I think we all knew something was wrong. The gardener, the servant, and I all hurried toward the pool. The wind was causing gentle little waves to dance all across the water. And in the middle of this floated Gatsby, trailing a thin red line of blood behind him.

---

■Gad's Hill ギャッズヒル《地名》 ■on foot 徒歩で ■head out to 〜に向かう ■keep line open 回線を開いたままにする ■in case 万が一に備えて ■no longer もはや〜でない ■all across 〜中で

その後の警察の調べで、ジョージ・ウィルソンの足取りがわかった。修理工場からポート・ローズヴェルト、さらにギャッズ・ヒルへと、徒歩だけで移動していた。ギャッズ・ヒルではサンドイッチを買ったが、食べはしなかった。何人かの少年が、歩いているウィルソンを目撃していて、警察に「頭がおかしそうな人」だったと話している。午後2時半頃には、ウィルソンはウェスト・エッグにいて、誰かにギャツビーの家はどこか訪ねていた。つまりこのときには、ギャツビーの名前を知っていたのだ。

　午後2時に、ギャツビーは水着に着替えてプールに向かった。デイジーから電話があった場合に備えて、電話の回線を開いたままにしていた。僕が電話をしてもつながらなかったのはそのせいだ。でもデイジーからの電話はなかった。もしかしたら、ギャツビーも期待していなかったのかもしれない。電話がなくても構わない、そう思っていたのかもしれない。あの日ギャツビーは、かつての暖かな世界を失ったという思いで、プールに向かったのだと思う。たった1つの夢を追って、長く生きすぎた。その代償を払うときを彼は迎えていた。きっと、空を見上げ、見慣れない世界を目にしたに違いない。

　使用人の1人が銃声を聞いたが、何の音かはわからなかったと後で話した。僕は間もなく駆けつけたが、居合わせた誰もが何かおかしいと気づいていたと思う。庭師と使用人と僕は、急いでプールに行った。風がプール一面にかすかな波を立てていた。その真ん中に、ギャツビーは浮かんでいた。細く赤い血の線を引きながら。

It was when we were bringing Gatsby's body toward the house that the gardener noticed another body lying nearby in the grass. It was Wilson. He had shot himself too.

# 16

Even now, two years later, I still remember the few days after Gatsby's death as an endless string of police questions. I was surprised to find that I was the only person who knew anything about Gatsby at all. I was even more surprised to find that I was the only person who seemed to care that he was dead.

I called Daisy half an hour after we found his body. But she and Tom had gone away that afternoon, taking many bags with them.

"Did they leave an address where they could be reached?" I asked their servant on the phone.

"No, sir."

"Did they say when they'd be back?"

"No."

■string of 相次ぐ〜　■anything at all 何でも

みんなでギャツビーを家の中へ運び込もうとしたとき、庭師が少し離れた芝生にもう1つの死体を見つけた。銃で自殺したウィルソンだった。

# 16

　2年がたった今でも、ギャツビーが死んでからの数日間を思い出そうとすると、果てしなく続いた警察の取り調べが脳裏に浮かぶ。ギャツビーについて何かしら知っているのは僕しかいないということにまず驚かされたが、それより驚いたのは、彼の死を気にかけていそうな人間も僕だけだったということだ。

　死体を発見してから30分ほど後に、僕はデイジーに電話をかけた。だが、デイジーとトムは、その日の午後すでに、たくさんの荷物を持っていなくなっていた。

「行き先は聞いていませんか？」僕は2人の執事に電話でたずねた。
「いいえ」
「いつ戻るかはわかりますか？」
「わかりません」

"Do you have any idea where they are?"

"I don't know, sir."

I wanted to bring somebody to him—a friend, or someone he worked with, or an officer he knew in the war. Anybody would have been fine. I wanted to go into the room where his body lay and reassure him. I wanted to say, "Don't worry, Gatsby. I'll get somebody for you. I won't let you go through this alone." But there really was no one.

I couldn't reach Wolfsheim over the phone, so the next day I sent him a letter. I looked everywhere for Gatsby's parents' address but couldn't find anything. The only link to Gatsby's past was the picture of Dan Cody hanging on the wall.

It was on the third day after his death that a short letter from Minnesota arrived. It was signed Henry C. Gatz. It was Gatsby's father. He said he was coming immediately and to please delay the funeral until he arrived.

Gatsby's father soon arrived. He was a thin, old man who looked almost helpless. He had on a long, cheap jacket, even in the warmth of September. He could not stop shaking, so I asked him to come inside and gave him some food. But he couldn't eat anything.

"I saw it in the Chicago newspaper," he said. "It was all in there. I came right away."

---

■let ~ go through this alone ～を独りでいさせる　■over the phone 電話で
■link to ～に関連している　■hanging on the wall 壁にかかっている

「どこへ行ったか心当たりは？」

「いいえ、ありません」

僕は誰かをギャツビーのもとへ連れていってやりたかった——友人でも、仕事仲間でも、戦争中の仲間でもいい。誰だってよかった。彼の死体が置かれている部屋へ入って、こう言ってやりたかった。「心配いらないよ、ギャツビー。僕が誰かを見つけてくる。1人ぼっちのまま行かせたりしないから」でも本当に、誰もいなかった。

ウルフシャイムには電話で連絡がつかず、翌日に手紙を出した。それからギャツビーの両親の連絡先をあちこち探しまわったが、結局見つけられなかった。ギャツビーの過去につながる唯一のものは、壁にかかったダン・コーディーの写真だけだった。

ギャツビーの死から3日後、ミネソタ州から短い手紙が届いた。手紙にはヘンリー・C・ギャッツと署名されていた。ギャツビーの父親だった。すぐに向かうので、自分が行くまで葬儀を延期してほしい、と書かれていた。

間もなく、ギャツビーの父親が到着した。痩せた老人で、ひどく打ちひしがれているようだった。9月の暑い日にもかかわらず、安っぽい丈の長い上着を羽織っていた。震えが止まらないようなので、僕は中に入るように言い、食べ物をすすめた。でも彼は何も口にできなかった。

「シカゴの新聞で見ました」と彼は言った。「何もかも書いてありました。それですぐ飛んできたのです」

"I'm sorry," I said. "I didn't know how to reach you."

"The newspaper said it was a crazy man who shot him. He must have been very crazy."

"Would you like some coffee?" I asked.

"No, I'm fine, thank you," he said. "Where is Jimmy?"

I took him into the room where his son lay. I left him alone in there. After a while, Mr. Gatz came out, tears still rolling slowly down his cheeks. I tried to speak to him as softly as possible.

"I didn't know what kind of funeral you would like, Mr. Gatz," I said. "I thought you might want to take the body back West."

"Jimmy always liked it better here, in the East," Gatz said. "He rose up to his position in the East. He had a big future ahead of him. If he lived, he would have been a great man."

I said he must want some rest and showed him to a bedroom. He fell asleep immediately.

The morning of the funeral, I went to Wolfsheim's office in New York. He would, I thought, at the very least come to the funeral.

When I arrived at his office, a young woman answered the door and tried to turn me away.

"Nobody's here right now," she said roughly. "Try some other time."

---

■take ~ back ~を引き取る　■up to ~に至るまで　■ahead of ~の前方に　■at the very least せめて、最低でも　■turn ~ away ~を追い返す　■right now 現在

「すみません」僕は言った。「ご連絡するすべがなくて」

「新聞には気のふれた男があいつを撃ったと書いてあった。とんでもなく気がふれていたに違いない」

「コーヒーでも飲みませんか？」

「いや、けっこうです。ジミーはどこですか？」

僕は彼の息子が眠る部屋へ連れていき、2人きりにした。しばらくして部屋を出てきたギャッツ氏の目からは、涙がゆっくりと頬をこぼれ落ちていた。僕はできるだけ優しく声をかけた。

「ギャッツさん、あなたが葬儀をどうなさりたいかわからなかったんです。西部に息子さんを連れて帰られるのかとも思いまして」

「ジミーは昔からこっちが好きでしたよ。東部がね」ギャッツ氏が言った。「息子が身を立てたのも東部です。大きな未来が待っていただろうに。生きていれば、偉大な男になったはずだ」

僕は彼に少し休むように言い、寝室へ案内した。彼はすぐに眠りこんだ。

葬儀の朝、僕はニューヨークにあるウルフシャイムの事務所を訪ねた。彼なら、せめて葬儀には出席してくれると思ったからだ。

事務所に着くと、若い女が戸口に現われ、僕を追い返そうとした。

「ここには誰もいません」彼女は突き放すように言った。「出直してください」

But I could hear people behind her. I mentioned Gatsby's name and she changed her attitude.

"Oh, I'm sorry," she said. "Hold on." She brought Wolfsheim to the door, and he greeted me with open arms. He said it was a sad time for all of us and offered me a cigarette.

"I remember when I first met him," he said, lighting his cigarette. "He was so poor he didn't even have a change of clothes. He had to wear his army uniform everywhere. He came into a bar I was running and asked for a job. He hadn't eaten anything in a few days. I said, 'Come on, have some lunch with me.' So he sat down and ate four dollars worth of food in half an hour."

"Did you start him in the business?" I asked.

"Yes," he said. "I taught him everything."

"Now he's dead," I said after a moment. "You were his closest friend, so I know you will come to his funeral this afternoon."

Wolfsheim's eyes filled with tears. "I'd like to come," he said, "but I can't. The police and the law know who I am. I just can't go out there. They may know what kind of business Gatsby was doing, and I can't get mixed up in it. I'm sorry, but it has to be that way."

"There's nothing to get mixed up in," I said. "He's dead. It's over now."

"I'm sorry," said Wolfsheim. He took my hand and shook it.

■Hold on. お待ちください　■with open arms 大歓迎で　■ask for a job 求職する
■start someone in business ～を採用する　■get mixed up 巻き添えを食う　■it has to be that way そうしなければならない

しかし、女の背後から人の声が聞こえた。僕がギャツビーの名前を出すと、女の態度が変わった。
「あら、失礼しました。お待ちください」彼女はそう言うと、ウルフシャイムを呼んできた。彼は両手を広げて僕を出迎えた。われわれ誰もが悲しんでいると言い、僕に煙草を進めた。
「あの男に初めて会ったときのことを覚えているよ」ウルフシャイムは煙草に火を点けていった。「一文無しで服も買えず、いつも軍服を着ていた。ある日、私がやっていた酒場にやってきて、仕事はないかと聞いてきたんだ。2、3日のあいだ何も食べていなかったそうだ。よし、昼飯を一緒に食おう、と私は言った。するとあいつは、座って30分のうちに4ドル分もたいらげたよ」
「あなたが商売を始めさせたんですか？」僕は聞いた。
「そうだ。私がすべて教えてやった」
「その彼も亡くなりました」僕はしばらくして言った。「あなたは親友でしたから、午後の葬儀に来てくださいますよね」
　ウルフシャイムの目に涙が浮かんだ。「ぜひ行きたい」と彼は言った。「だが無理だ。警察や司法機関は私の正体を知っている。だから表へは出ていけない。やつらはギャツビーがどんな商売をしていたか知っているかもしれない。そこで巻き込まれるわけにはいかないんだ。申し訳ないが、他にどうしようもないんだよ」
「巻き込まれるも何もないでしょう」僕は言った。「彼は死んだ。すべて終わったんです」
「すまない」ウルフシャイムは言って、僕の手を握った。

When I left Wolfsheim's office, the sky had turned dark and it was beginning to rain. When I arrived at Gatsby's house, I saw Mr. Gatz walking through the halls excitedly. His pride in his son and his wealth was increasing.

He came up to me and said he had something to show me. It was a photograph of Gatsby's house. The paper was bent at the corners from many hands touching it. I think he had shown it to people so often that it was more real to him now than the actual house itself.

"Jimmy sent me this picture," he said. "Look there, isn't it a very pretty picture?"

"Very pretty," I said. "Did you see him lately?"

"Jimmy came to see me two years ago. He bought me the house I live in now. We were very sad when he ran away from home, but now I see it was all for a reason. He knew he had a big future in front of him. And ever since he made his success, he was very generous with me."

Then he pulled something else out of his pocket. It was an old children's book.

■run away 家出する　■ever since ～以来ずっと　■be generous with ～に対して寛容だ　■pull ～ out of ～を引っ張り出す

ウルフシャイムの事務所を出ると、空が暗くなっていて、雨が降りはじめた。ギャツビーの家に着くと、ギャッツ氏が興奮した様子でホールを歩き回っていた。息子とその財産を誇りに思う気持ちが高まっているようだった。
　ギャッツ氏は僕のところへやってきて、見せたいものがあると言った。それはギャツビー邸の写真だった。写真は、たくさんの人の手に触れて四隅が折れ曲がっていた。しょっちゅう人に見せていたから、彼にとっては実際の家よりも現実味があるのだろう。

「ジミーがこの写真を送ってきてくれたんです」彼は言った。「見てください、きれいに撮れているでしょう？」
「実にきれいですね」僕は言った。「最近、息子さんに会いましたか？」
「2年前に来てくれました。いま私が住んでいる家を買ってくれたんです。息子が家を出ていったとき、私らはひどく悲しんだ。でも今は、すべて理由があってのことだったとわかります。息子は自分に大きな未来が待っているとわかっていたんでしょう。そして成功してからは、私にとてもよくしてくれました」
　それから彼は、ポケットからまた何かを取り出した。古びた子ども向けの本だ。

"This was Jimmy's," he said. He opened the book to the last page and showed me a list written in pencil. It read:

SCHEDULE, SEPTEMBER 12, 1906

Rise from bed.....6 a.m.
Exercise.....6:15-6:30 a.m.
Study electricity, etc......7:15-8:15 a.m.
Work.....8:30-4:30 p.m.
Baseball and sports.....4:30-5:00 p.m.
Practice speaking and poise.....5:00-6:00 p.m.
Study.....7:00-9:00 p.m.

GOALS

No wasting time
No more smoking
Bath every other day
Read one book or magazine per week
Save $5.00 [crossed out] $3.00 per week
Be better to parents

■poise 図 立ち居振る舞い　■every other day 1日おきに　■cross out（文字などを）線を引いて消す

「これはジミーのものです」彼はそう言って、本の裏表紙を開き、鉛筆で書かれたリストを見せてくれた。そこにはこう書かれていた——

時間割　1906年9月12日

起床　　　　　　　　　午前6時
体操　　　　　　　　　午前6時15分〜6時30分
電気その他の勉強　　　午前7時15分〜8時15分
仕事　　　　　　　　　午前8時30分〜午後4時30分
野球その他のスポーツ　午後4時30分〜5時
演説と所作の練習　　　午後5時〜6時
勉強　　　　　　　　　午後7時〜9時


目標

時間を無駄にしない
煙草をやめる
1日おきに入浴する
毎週、本または雑誌を1冊読む
毎週5ドル（バツ印で消して）3ドルを貯金する
両親にもっとよくする

A little before three o'clock, the minister came. I began to look out the window for arriving cars. So did Gatsby's father. We waited a while, then the servants gathered, and the minister said it was time to head out. Mr. Gatz said he worried the rain would keep people away. I took the minister aside and asked him to wait another half hour. But it was useless. Nobody came.

At the funeral, Gatsby was buried in the rain. And I remembered without anger or any emotion that Daisy never sent a letter or flowers.

■So did ~. ~も同様にした  ■head out 出発する  ■keep ~ away ~の足を遠のける  ■take ~ aside ~をそばに呼ぶ

3時少し前に牧師がやってきた。僕は窓の外を見て、車が来ないか気にしはじめた。ギャツビーの父親も同じだった。僕たちはそうやってしばらく待ったが、使用人たちが集まって、牧師がもう時間ですと言った。ギャッツ氏は雨のせいで人が来れないのではと心配した。僕は牧師を脇に連れていき、もう30分待ってほしいと頼んだ。だが無駄だった。誰も来なかったのだ。
　雨が降る中、ギャツビーは埋葬された。僕は怒りも何も感じずに、デイジーがついに1通の手紙も花束もよこさなかったことを思い出した。

# 17

I see now that this has been a story about the West after all. Tom and Gatsby, Daisy and Jordan and I, we all came from the West. Perhaps we all lacked something that made us suitable for life in the East.

Even when the East excited me the most, things still felt a little wrong to me. There was too much action in the East, too much wealth, and too many people caring too little about each other. After Gatsby's death, I didn't want to live in the East anymore. So I decided to go home to the West.

I met Jordan Baker one last time. After the night that Myrtle Wilson died, I knew I could never be with Jordan. She also knew then that it was over between us. But I didn't want to leave without saying sorry. She listened to me, but I don't think she forgave me.

■after all 結局のところ　■it is over between us 私たちの仲はもう終わりだ

# 17

　この話はつまるところ、西部についての物語だったのだと今では思う。トムにギャツビー、デイジー、それに僕とジョーダンも、西部の出身だ。きっと僕たちはみんな、東部での暮らしに馴染むための何かが欠けていたのだろう。

　東部に胸を躍らせていたときでさえ、僕の中ではどこかしっくりしない感覚があった。東部は、やたら目まぐるしく、富で溢れかえり、おびただしい数の人が互いにまるで気遣うことなく行き交う場所だ。ギャツビーが死んでしまってからは、僕はこれ以上東部では暮らしたくないと思った。そして、西部に帰ることを決めた。

　最後に一度だけ、ジョーダン・ベイカーに会った。マートル・ウィルソンが死んだあの夜を境に、ジョーダンとは一緒になれないと気づいた。彼女もあのとき、僕たちの関係が終わったことに気づいたと思う。でも僕は、去る前に彼女に謝っておきたかった。彼女は話に耳を傾けてくれたが、僕を許してくれたとは思わない。

One afternoon in late October, a few days before I left, I saw Tom Buchanan. He was walking ahead of me along Fifth Avenue. When he turned to look in a store window, he saw me, and I couldn't get away.

"What's the matter, Nick?" he asked, walking toward me with his hand out. "Don't you want to shake hands with me?"

"No, I don't," I said. "You know what I think of you."

"You're crazy, Nick," he said.

"Tom, what did you tell George Wilson that afternoon? I know he must have found you and talked to you. I know you must have given him Gatsby's name."

Tom stared at me, and I knew I had guessed correctly. As George Wilson walked through Long Island searching for the man with the yellow car, it was Tom who had told him the car was Gatsby's. I started to turn away, but Tom stopped me.

"I told him the truth," he said. "He came to my door while we were getting ready to leave. He tried to force his way in. He was crazy enough to kill me if I hadn't told him who owned the car. Anyway, Gatsby tricked us all! He was a criminal too, and he got what he deserved. He ran over Myrtle like he was running over a dog, and he never even stopped his car."

I was so shocked I didn't know what to say. Daisy hadn't told him the truth.

---

■get away 逃げる、免れる ■with one's hand out 片手を出して ■turn away 背を向ける ■force one's way in 強行突破する ■run over ～を車でひく

10月後半のある日の午後、東部を発つ数日前に、トム・ブキャナンに出くわした。彼は5番街で僕の少し先を歩いていた。ある店のウィンドウをのぞこうとした拍子に僕に気づき、僕は逃げようがなかった。

　「どうしたんだ、ニック？」彼は僕の方に歩いてきて、手を差し出した。「僕と握手するのも嫌か？」
　「ああ、嫌だね」僕は言った。「きみをどう思っているかは知ってるだろう」
　「どうかしてるぞ、ニック」
　「トム、あの日の午後、ジョージ・ウィルソンに何を言った？ あの男がきみを見つけ出して、話しに行ったのはわかっている。ギャツビーの名前を教えたのはきみなんだろう」
　トムは僕をじっと見つめた。それで、僕の推測が正しかったとわかった。黄色い車の持ち主を探してロングアイランドを歩き回っていたジョージ・ウィルソンに、ギャツビーの車だと教えたのはトムだったのだ。僕は背を向けて歩き出そうとしたが、トムに止められた。
　「僕はあいつに真実を話したんだ」彼は言った。「あいつは、僕らが家を出る準備をしていたところにやってきた。無理やり中に入ってこようとしたよ。ひどく逆上していて、車の持ち主を教えなければこっちが殺されそうな勢いだった。そもそも、ギャツビーが僕たちをだましたんだ！ あいつも犯罪者なんだから、自業自得だ。まるで犬みたいにマートルを轢いておいて、車を止めもしなかったんだぞ」
　僕は驚きのあまり何も言えなかった。デイジーはトムに真実を話していないのだ。

"That's not true," I managed to say.

"And I suffered too," said Tom. "After Myrtle died, I went to our apartment in the city. I saw her little dog sitting there, and I just cried like a baby. It was awful."

I could never forgive or like Tom. But I saw that in his mind, he had done nothing wrong. I realized finally that Tom and Daisy were careless people. They destroyed things and people and then just walked back into the safety of their money. They left other people to clean everything up. I gave up being angry and shook Tom's hand. I knew I would never see him again.

On my last night in Long Island, I went over to Gatsby's empty house. I looked at it one last time and then wandered down to the beach. I sat on the sand. I looked up at the stars and began to imagine Long Island as it would have looked to the first European sailors who saw it. Instead of Gatsby's house, there would have been trees here, and instead of a city, there would have been a forest. I thought about that old world, and I thought about Gatsby when he first saw the green light at the end of Daisy's dock. It was his discovery—he had finally come to a world where he could reach his dreams. What he didn't realize was that his dreams were always moving further into the past. But he kept reaching toward the future. And so do we all. As we continue to reach forward, we move further into the past.

---

■do nothing wrong 何１つ間違ったことはしていない  ■clean everything up 全部片付ける  ■one last time 最後にもう一度だけ  ■reach one's dream 夢に手が届く

「それは違う」そう言うのがやっとだった。

「僕だって苦しんだんだ」トムは言った。「マートルが死んだ後、ニューヨークのアパートメントに行った。そうしたら彼女の子犬がそこにいて、僕は赤ん坊みたいに泣いたよ。たまらなくつらかった」

トムを許すことも、好きになることも僕にはできなかった。でも、トム自身は何も悪いことはしていないと思っているのが、見てとれた。トムとデイジーがぞんざいな人間であることに、僕はようやく気がついた。色んなものや人をめちゃくちゃに壊して、自分たちは財産という安全な場所へ帰っていく。後始末は他人まかせだ。僕は怒る気もなくなって、トムと握手をした。もう2度と会うことはないと思った。

ロングアイランドで過ごす最後の夜、空き家になったギャツビーの家に行ってみた。最後にもう1度家を眺め、浜辺に向かって歩いた。砂浜に座って星空を見上げ、ヨーロッパから来た船乗りが初めて目にしたロングアイランドを思い描いた。きっと、ギャツビー邸のかわりに木々が生え、町のかわりに森が茂っていたに違いない。僕はその古い世界を思い、デイジーの家の桟橋の端に光る緑の灯りを初めて見たときのギャツビーを思った。それは彼にとって発見だった——ついに自分の夢がかなう世界へたどり着いたのだ。彼が気づかなかったのは、その夢がつねに過去へ遠ざかっていくものだったということだ。でも彼は、未来に向かって手を伸ばしつづけた。それは僕たちも同じだ。絶えず前に進もうとしながら、過去へ押し流されているのだから。

# 覚えておきたい英語表現

> He did very well in the war, but all he wanted to do after the war was to go back home. (p.188, 5行目)
> 
> 彼は戦場でとてもよく活躍した。しかし、戦争が終わった時に彼が求めていたことは、家に帰る、それだけだった。

【解説】do well で「うまくやる」という意味です。この場合、他国から勲章をもらうほど活躍したことを表します。

"All A want to do is ~ ." は直訳すると、「Aがしたいと思っていることの全ては~だ」となります。つまり「ただひたすら~したいだけ」「~することしかのぞんでいない」という意味になります。

遠いヨーロッパの戦場で英雄的な活躍をしたギャツビーでしたが、恋においてその努力が報われることはありませんでした。帰国した彼を待っていたのは、第一次大戦後のバブル景気に沸く祖国と国民でした。先の大戦で工業先進国ドイツを追い落としたアメリカに、ジャズエイジと呼ばれる華やかな時代が訪れます。自動車やラジオなどが急速に普及し、大量生産・大量消費の時代が到来したのです。

世界が経験した初の大戦で、あまりに多くの死と向き合った若者たち。かろうじて命をつなぎ止め、帰国した彼らを待っていたのは、戦場での経験とはあまりにかけ離れた繁栄に狂乱する祖国の姿でした。急速な近代化も相まって、今までの価値観を打ち崩されるような経験をした若者たちが「ロストジェネレーション」と呼ばれる世代です。その中からフィッツジェラルド、ヘミングウェイなど著名な作家が生まれました。

ギャツビーもニックも戦争経験者です。しかし、彼らが国のために命を張っていた間に、トムやデイジーたち金持ち階級はどこで何をしていたでしょうか?

ニックは最終的にギャツビーと親友と呼べる仲になります。トムとデイジーやベイカーなど、戦争を経験していない人たちとは最終的に心を許せる仲になれなかったのはこんなところにも伏線があるのではないでしょうか。ロストジェネレーションにとって、「戦争」は大きな意味を持ちます。

> Gatsby could only offer her promises, while Tom offered her reality. (p.188, 15行目)
> ギャツビーは彼女に約束しか与えることはできなかったが、一方でトムは彼女に現実をもたらしたのだ。

**【解説】** whileは「〜の間に」という意味もありますが、ここでは「一方では」という意味で使われています。貧しかったギャツビーは、デイジーに形ある物を与えることはできませんでした。しかしトムは富豪で十分なお金がありました。いつ帰ってくるか分からないギャツビーよりも、目の前にいる財力を持ったトムのほうをデイジーは選びます。デイジーの「結婚した」という手紙を受け取った後、帰国し2人の思い出の場所を巡ったギャツビーの心境は詳しく書かれていません。そこがかえってギャツビーの悲しみを強調しているかのようです。

　promiseよりもrealityを選んだデイジー。当時の女性、とくに上流階級の女性にはそんな生き方しか選べなかったのかもしれません。一概には非難できないことでしょう。promiseとrealityという言葉が持つ意味とその重さを考えさせられる文章です。

> Then he went to New York to make his fortune. (p.188, 下から2行目)
> そして彼は一財産つくるためにニューヨークへ向かった。

**【解説】** fortuneには大きく、「財産・富」と「運命」という2つの意味があります。make fortuneという組み合わせで作る場合、「一財産築く」という意味です。しかし、fortuneに「運命」という意味もあることを頭に入れてこの文章を読むと、ギャツビーの心に近づける気がしませんか？

> You're worth more than the whole bunch of them!
> （p.190, 下から6行目）
>
> 君はあの連中全員よりも価値のある人間だよ！

【解説】be worthで「価値がある」という意味です。more than 〜は比較級で「〜以上に」という意味です。bunch of 〜とは「〜の束」とか「〜の山」、「一房」などの意味がありますが、人や動物に対しても「群れ・一味」といった意味で使えます。

　bunch of 〜には「あの連中」という感じの、軽蔑に近いニュアンスが含まれます。ニックがだれのことを指しているかもう分かりますよね？

　"I've always been glad I said that.（僕はあの言葉を言っておいて良かったと常々思う）"というニックも言っていますが、この台詞はギャツビーだけでなく我々読者も「言っておいてくれてありがとうニック！」と思うのではないでしょうか？

> It was useless. Nobody came.（p.212, 6行目）
>
> それは無駄だった。誰も来なかったのだ。

【解説】ギャツビーの葬式には、ニック、ギャツビーの父、使用人、牧師しか来ませんでした。ニックはデイジーが手紙や花すら送って来なかったことに、もはや何の感情も抱いていません。

　自分の身代わりとなって殺されたギャツビーに知らんぷりを決め込んだデイジー、ウィルソンをそそのかして「邪魔な」ギャツビーを殺させたトム、そのどちらにもニックは愛想を尽かしています。上述の台詞の意味がここでも思い出されます。

　以前にはギャツビー邸での華やかなパーティーには、たくさんの人が来ていました。しかし、ゲストの多くがギャツビー氏本人のことを知らない、顔も見たことのない人たちでした。誰が招待主なのか分からないまま、饗宴をひたすら楽しむ。まるで中身のない虚栄そのものです。あんなに来ていたゲストが誰一人、葬式に来ていないことが、ギャツビー邸でのパーティーがいかに空虚なものだったかを示しています。

　ロストジェネレーション世代の目には、当時のアメリカの繁栄ぶりもこんなふうに映っていたのかもしれませんね。

> They destroyed things and people and then just walked back into the safety of their money. (p.218, 7行目)
> 彼らは物事や人を破壊し、そして金の詰まった金庫に戻るだけなのだ。

【解説】ニックがトムとデイジーを「不注意な人間なのだ」と評した後に言う言葉です。ギャツビー、ウィルソン、マートルといった「貧乏人(元貧乏人)」がトムとデイジーに振り回された末の結末を思い出してみてください。ニックとベイカーが「不注意な運転」について話をしているところも読み返してみるとよいでしょう。

> But he kept reaching toward the future. And so do we all. (p.218, 下から3行目)
> しかし彼は未来をつかもうとし続けていた。そして僕らも皆そうなのだ。

【解説】reachは、ボクシング用語の「リーチ」を思い出させますが、多義な言葉です。「(到着地に) 着く、手を伸ばして〜を取る、〜に到達する」など多くの意味を持っています。語義は「手を差し出す」なので、そこから単語のイメージを広げると状況に応じた訳ができると思います。

　人は未来を追い求めても、過去へ過去へと大きな力で押し流されてしまうものです。ギャツビーはそのことに気付いていませんでした。彼は一途に夢(＝未来)をつかもうと奮闘し続けてきました。ニックはそんなギャツビーの姿から、今後の人生の指針のようなものを感じ取ったのかもしれません。

　孤独に見えたギャツビー、そしてこちらも孤独な存在だったニックは、最後に分かりあえます。解釈の仕方は人それぞれですが、グレートギャツビーの最後を読むと、ロストジェネレーション世代の若者たちが、現実に絶望していたかに見えて、実は希望ある未来を心のどこかで追い求め、もがいていたように思えませんか。多くの人を魅了してやまない、物語最後の段落をじっくり味わってください。

**E-CAT**

**E**nglish **C**onversational **A**bility **T**est
国際英語会話能力検定

● E-CATとは…
英語が話せるようになるための
テストです。インターネット
ベースで、30分であなたの発
話力をチェックします。

www.ecatexam.com

● iTEP®とは…
世界各国の企業、政府機関、アメリカの大学
300校以上が、英語能力判定テストとして採用。
オンラインによる90分のテストで文法、リー
ディング、リスニング、ライティング、スピー
キングの5技能をスコア化。iTEP®は、留学、就
職、海外赴任などに必要な、世界に通用する英
語力を総合的に評価する画期的なテストです。

www.itepexamjapan.com

---

[IBC対訳ライブラリー]
**英語で読むグレート・ギャツビー**

2013年6月4日　第1刷発行
2021年3月22日　第3刷発行

原著者　　F・スコット・フィッツジェラルド

発行者　　浦　　晋亮

発行所　　IBCパブリッシング株式会社
　　　　　〒162-0804 東京都新宿区中里町29番3号 菱秀神楽坂ビル9F
　　　　　Tel. 03-3513-4511　Fax. 03-3513-4512
　　　　　www.ibcpub.co.jp

印刷所　　株式会社シナノパブリッシングプレス
CDプレス　株式会社ケーエヌコーポレーションジャパン

© IBC Publishing, Inc. 2013

Printed in Japan

落丁本・乱丁本は、小社宛にお送りください。送料小社負担にてお取り替えいたします。
本書の無断複写（コピー）は著作権法上での例外を除き禁じられています。

ISBN978-4-7946-0209-1